Exploring Our Faith Through CRAFTS

LYNN BRISSON

Abingdon Press

CONTENTS

Cornucopia...4

Easter Lilies...7

Christmas Angel...9

Noah's Ark...16

A Gift for Someone Special...19

God's Rainbow...21

Friendly Frog...23

Stained-glass Window...26

Share Bear Sack...28

Chick...30

The Creation...33

Christ Is Born...36

Daniel in the Lion's Den...39

Jonah and the Whale...42

Hot Air Balloon...44

Dove...46

Owl...49

Fall Activity...52

Snowman...53

Spring Activity...55

God's Little Summer Creatures...57

Bible Bookmark...59

Little Lamb...60

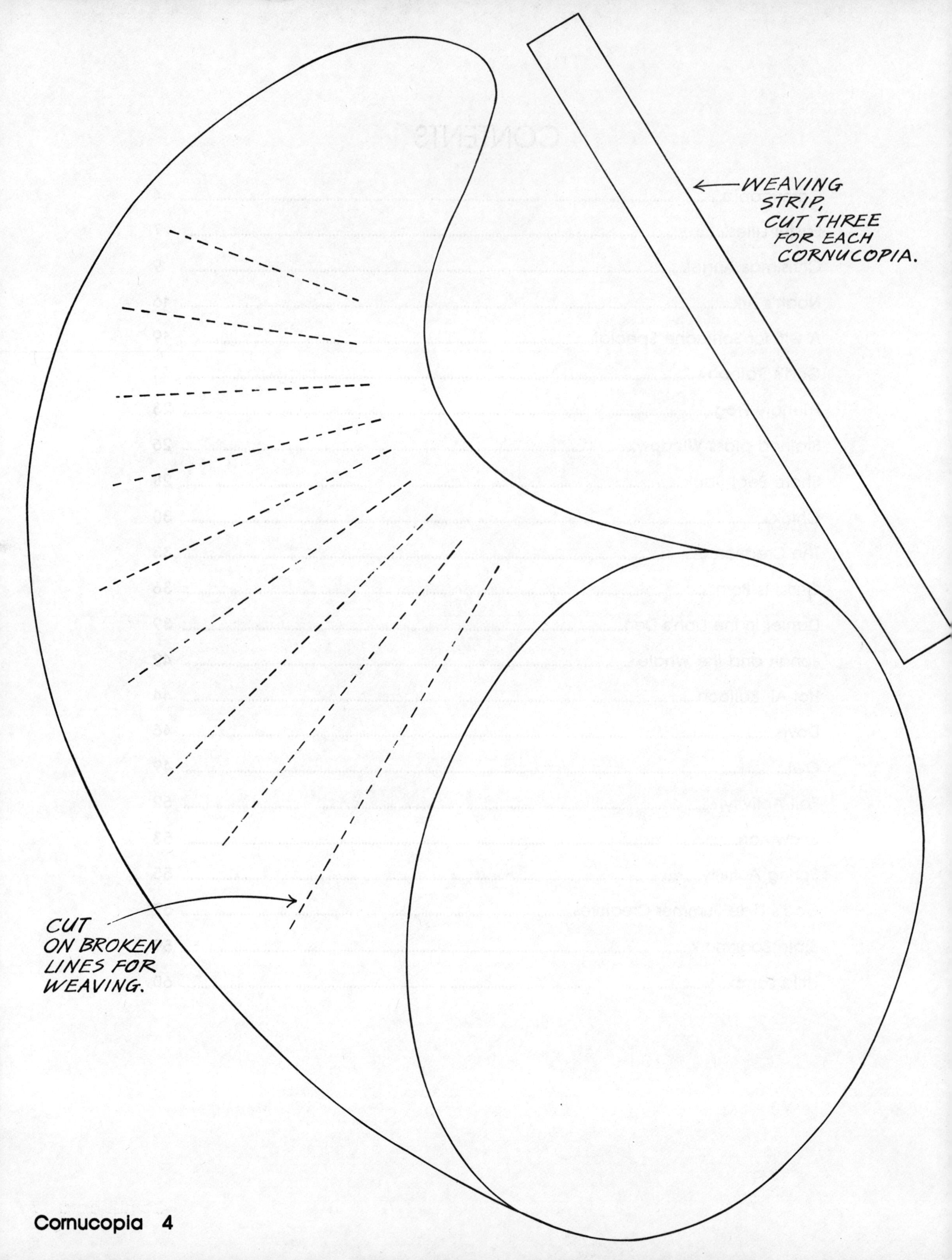

WEAVING STRIP, CUT THREE FOR EACH CORNUCOPIA.
CUT ON BROKEN LINES FOR WEAVING.

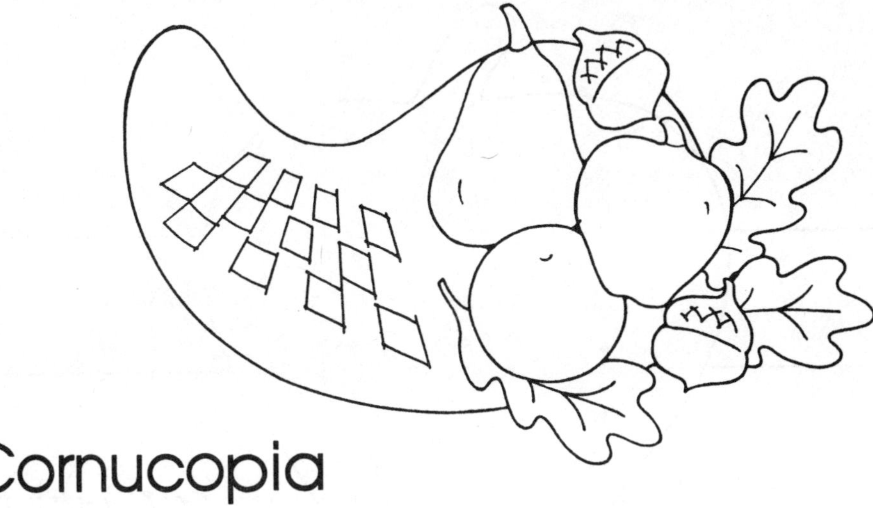

Cornucopia

The children will have fun making a cornucopia filled with three-dimensional fruit for the Thanksgiving season.

MATERIALS:

construction paper

crayons

scissors

glue

CONSTRUCTION:

1. Reproduce patterns.

2. Color and cut out.

3. Cut tabs along dotted lines. Fold tabs back and slot together.

4. Place glue on tabs and glue the three-dimensional fruit to the cornucopia.

5. If desired, basket may be woven. Cut 3 strips from same color paper as basket.

6. Cut slots in basket and weave each strip over and under through basket.

7. Trim each strip and glue in place.

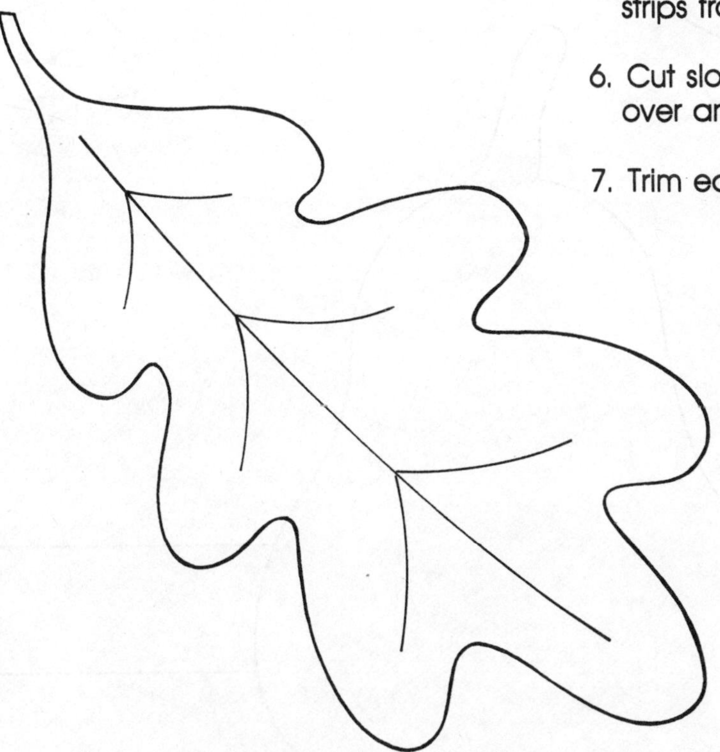

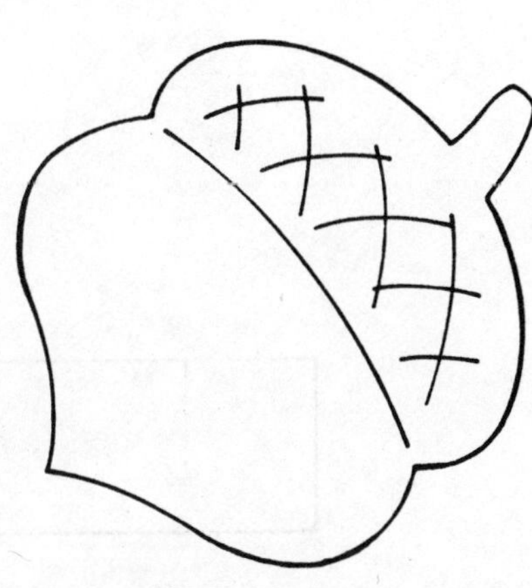

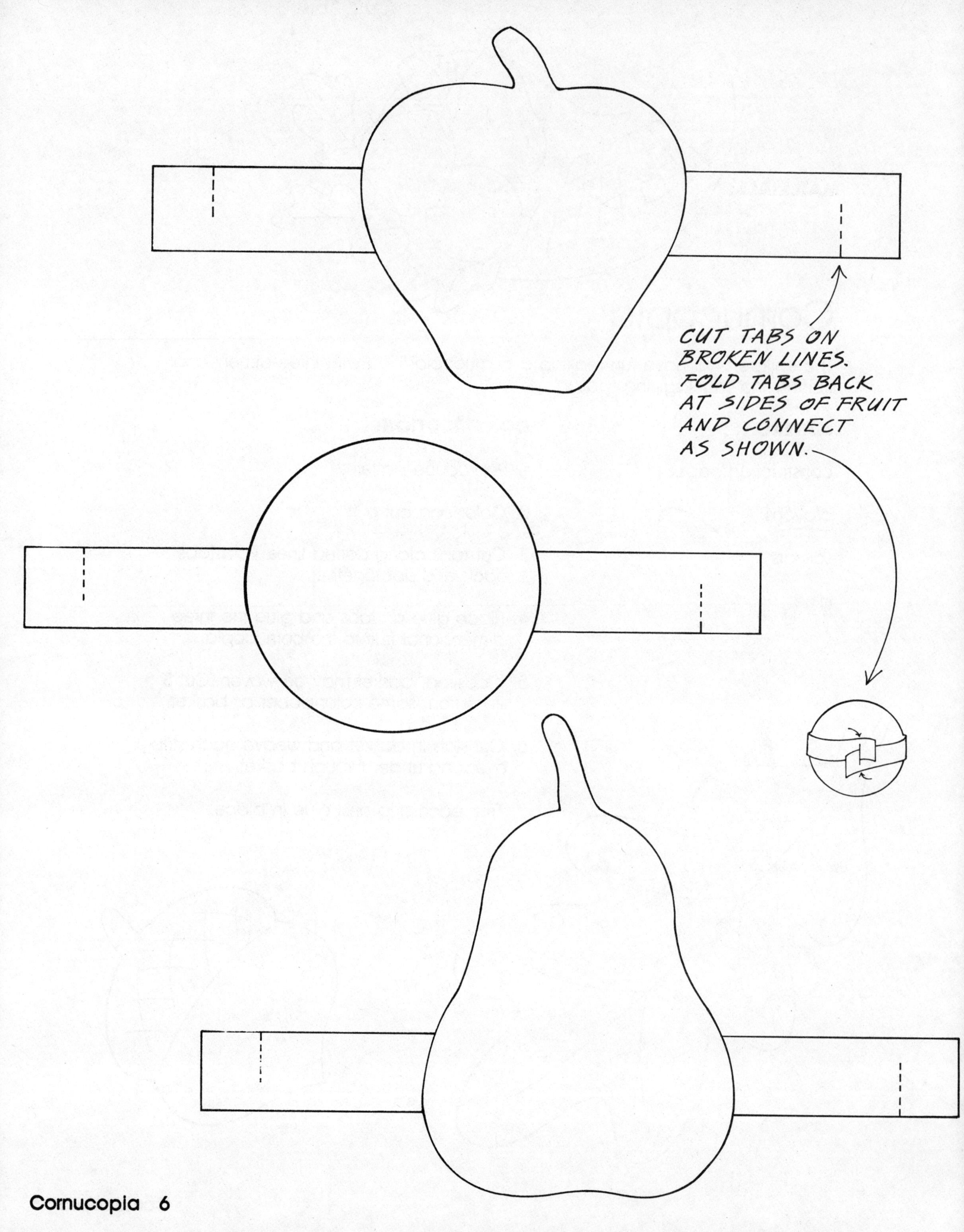

CUT TABS ON
BROKEN LINES.
FOLD TABS BACK
AT SIDES OF FRUIT
AND CONNECT
AS SHOWN.

Easter Lilies

Lilies are a lovely way to express the Easter season. Let the children make several of these lilies.

MATERIALS:

construction paper

12" green pipe cleaners

12" yellow pipe cleaners

stapler

scissors

glue

CONSTRUCTION:

1. Reproduce patterns.

2. Cut out patterns.

3. Cut a 12" yellow pipe cleaner into thirds. This will be the stamens.

4. Twist the green pipe cleaner around the three yellow pipe cleaners (stamens).

5. Fold the bottom part of the lily around the stamens and the green pipe cleaner (stem), then staple.

6. Curl lily petals out with a pencil.

7. Staple two leaves to the pipe cleaner.

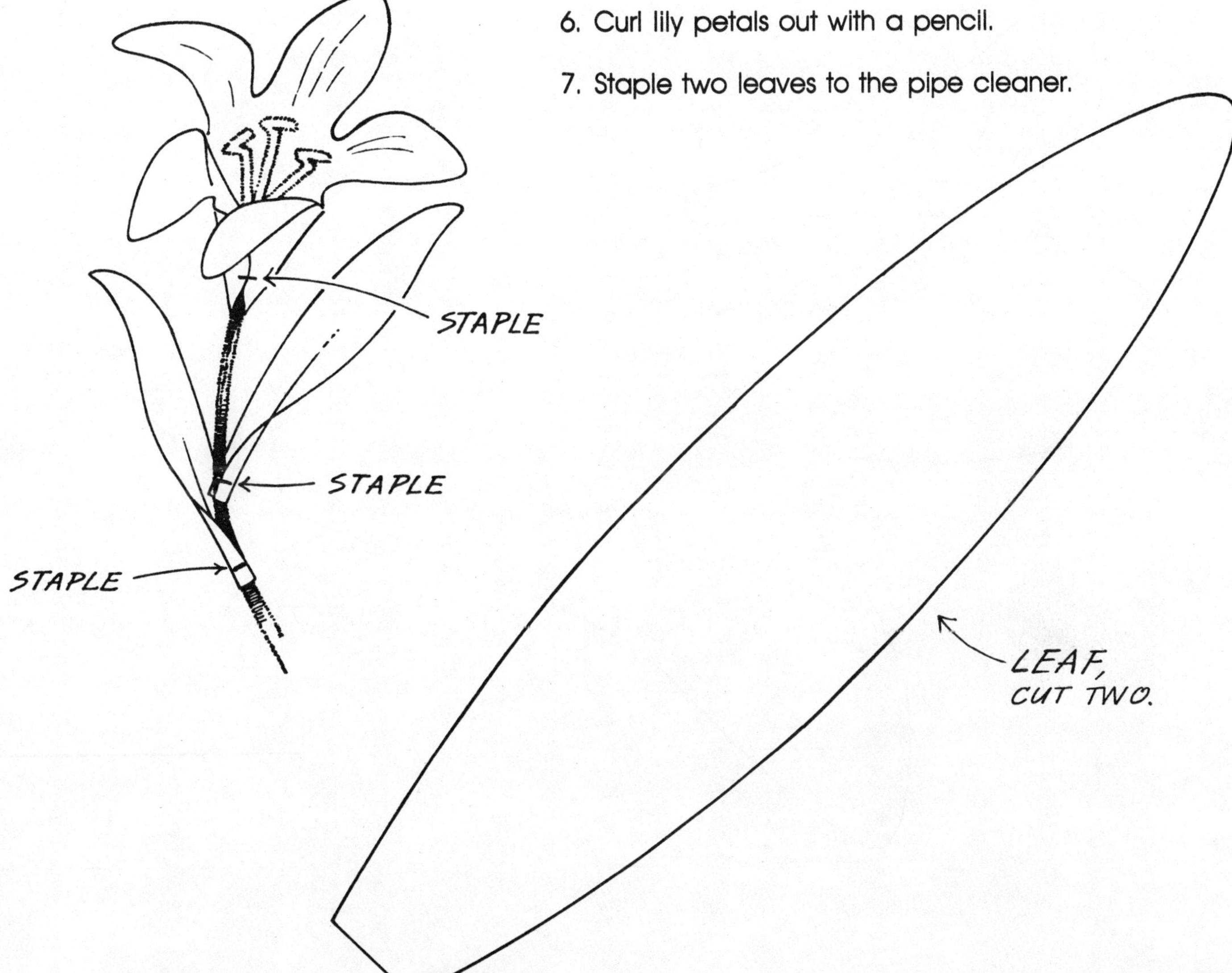

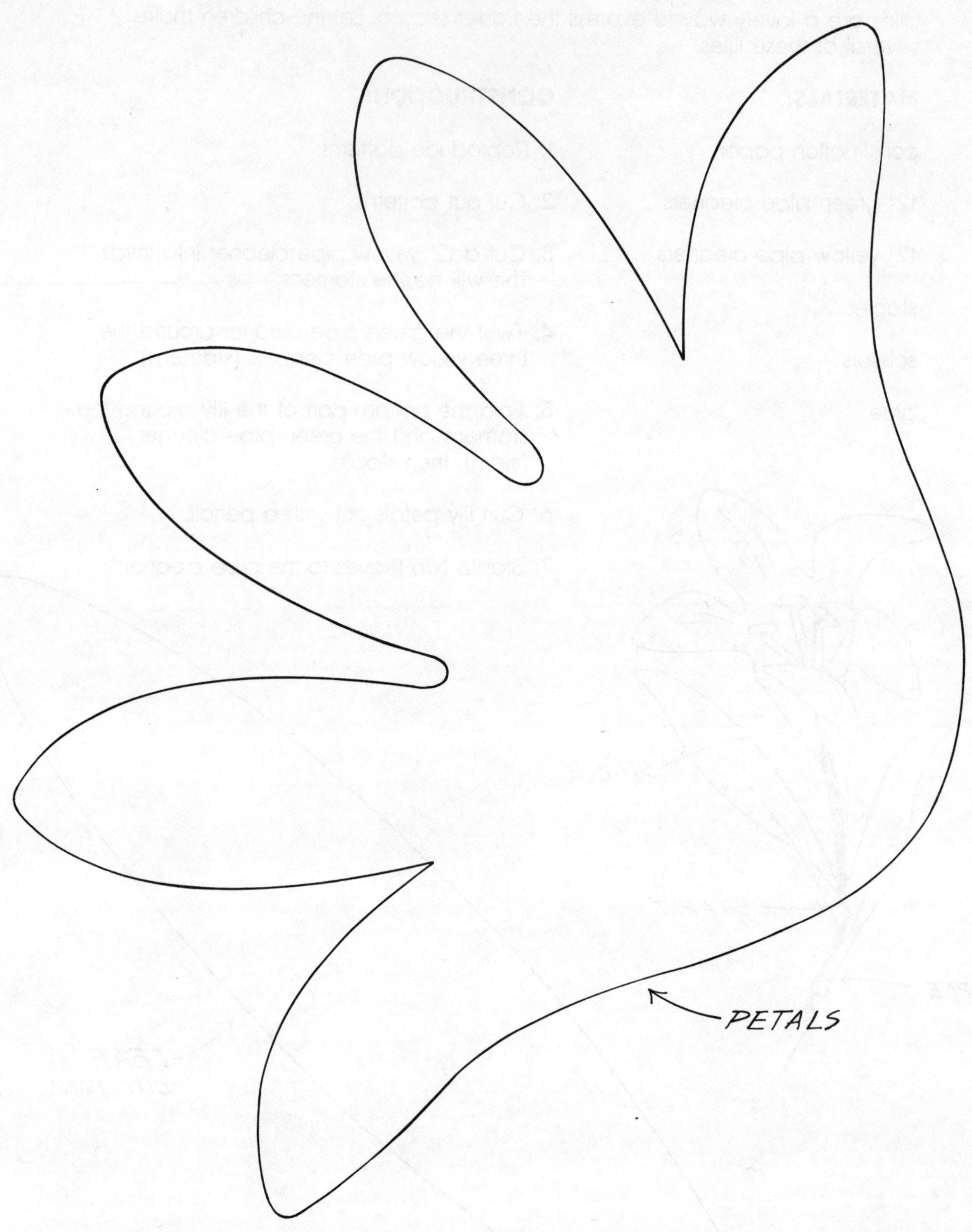
PETALS

Christmas Angel

Here is a delightful little stand-up angel decoration for the Christmas season. A larger pattern is provided for the teacher. It can be used for the bulletin board or the door.

MATERIALS:

construction paper

yellow pipe cleaners (cut to 5½")

cotton balls

crystal glitter

scissors

glue

tape

CONSTRUCTION:

1. Reproduce patterns.

2. Color and cut out.

3. Overlap the two sides of the angel pattern, then glue.

4. Twist the pipe cleaner to form a halo. Place halo over backside of tab, then fold tab back and glue.

5. If desired, spread glue over the wings and sprinkle with crystal glitter. Glue wings to angel.

6. Place glue on tabs of the angel pattern, fold tabs under, then glue to the cloud.

7. Pull the cotton balls apart and glue to the cloud.

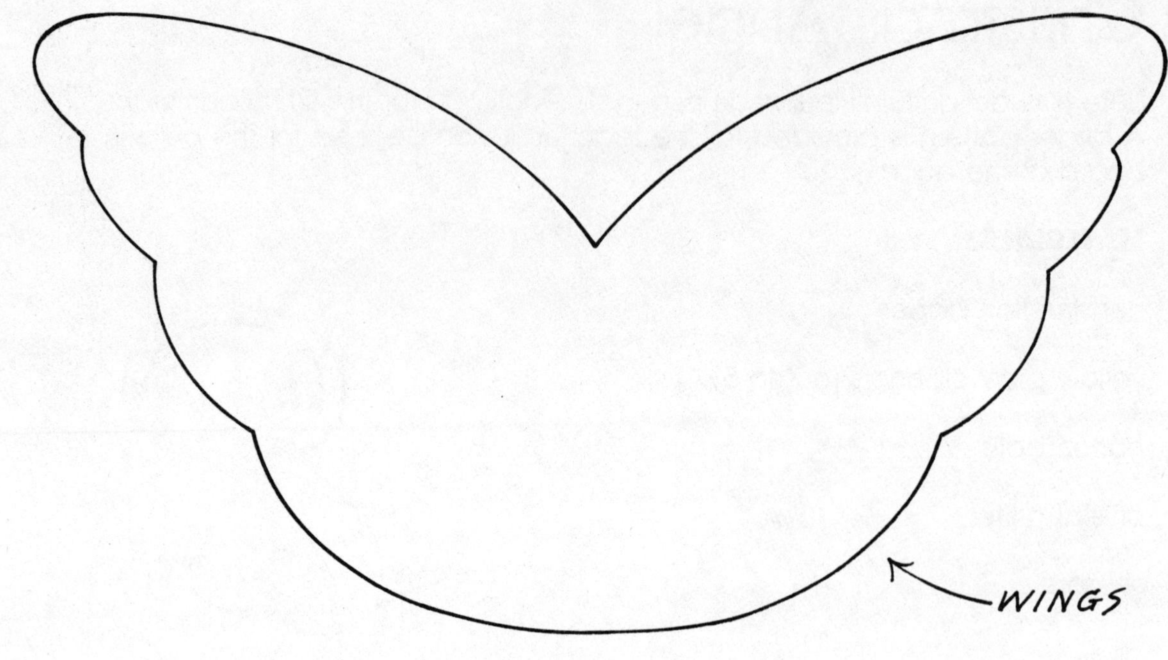

Angel 10

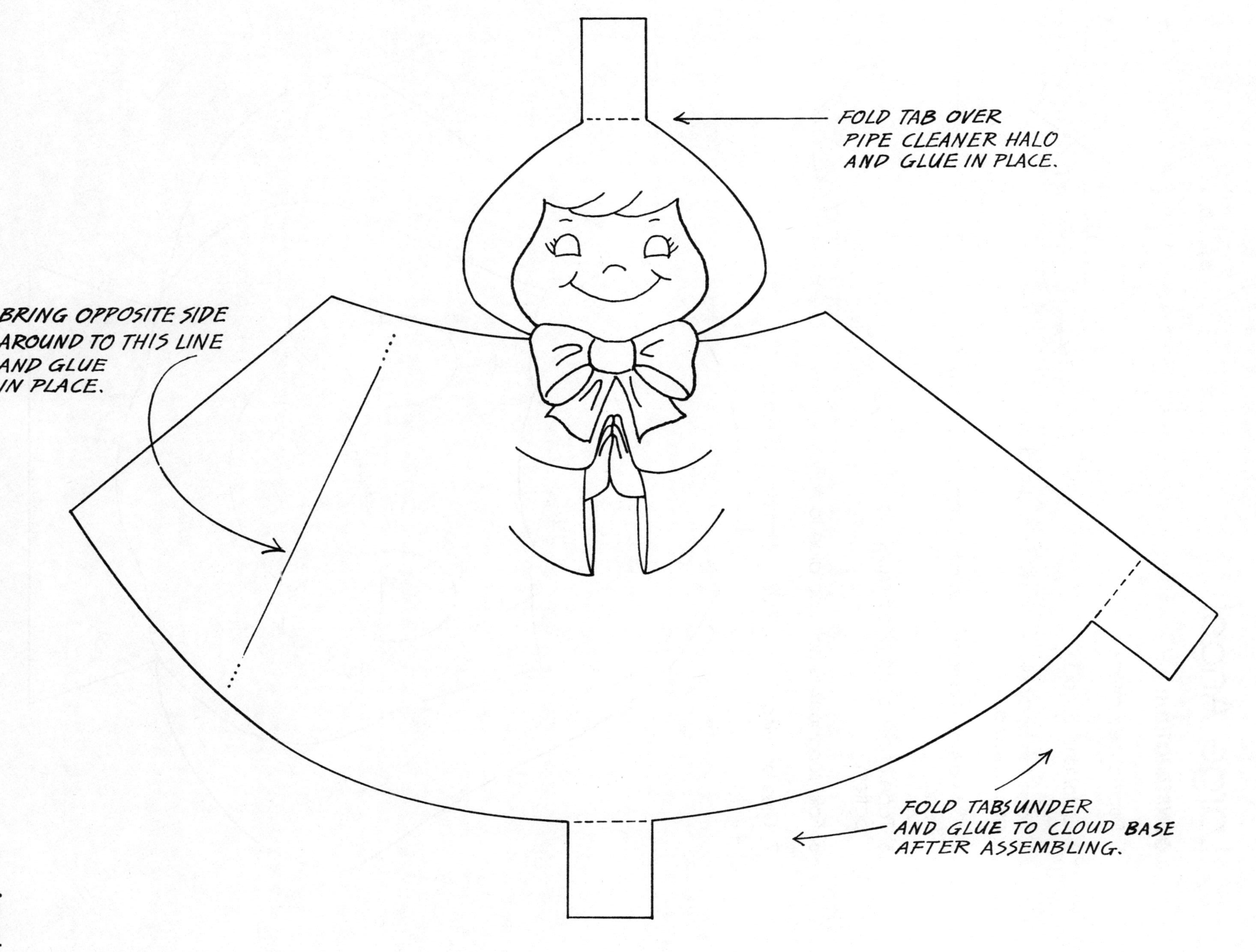

FOLD TAB OVER PIPE CLEANER HALO AND GLUE IN PLACE.
BRING OPPOSITE SIDE AROUND TO THIS LINE AND GLUE IN PLACE.
FOLD TABS UNDER AND GLUE TO CLOUD BASE AFTER ASSEMBLING.

Large Angel

CONSTRUCTION:

1. Reproduce patterns.

2. Color and cut out.

3. Tape the body pieces together and fold arms forward.

4. Cut slots on shoulders and insert angel's head.

5. Tape angel to the cloud as indicated on pattern.

6. Fold songbook in half and glue to hands.

7. Glue on wings.   8. Glue cotton balls to cloud.

— CUT TWO —
CUT
FOLD ON THIS LINE
TAPE TOGETHER ON BACK.
FOLD FORWARD

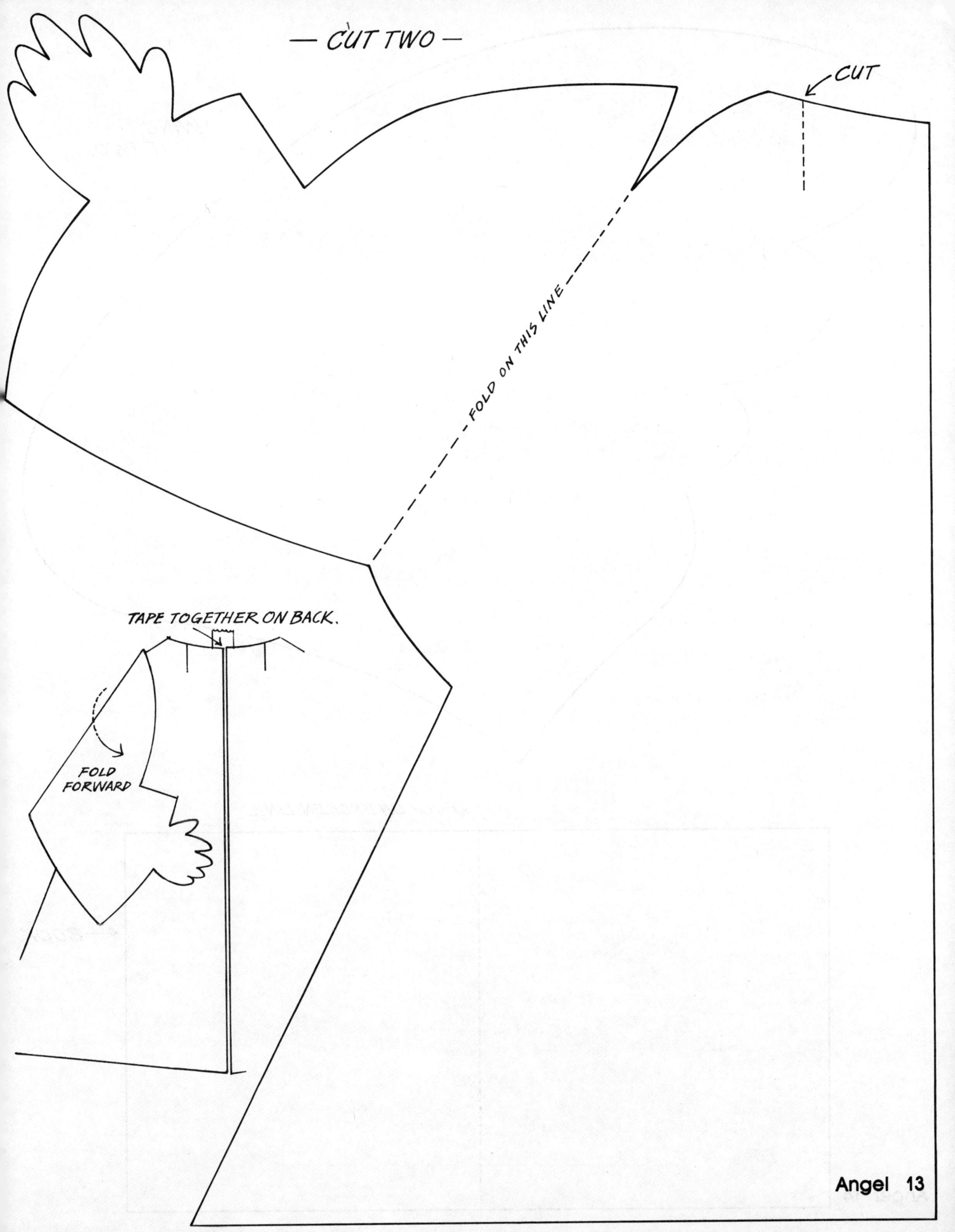

Angel 13

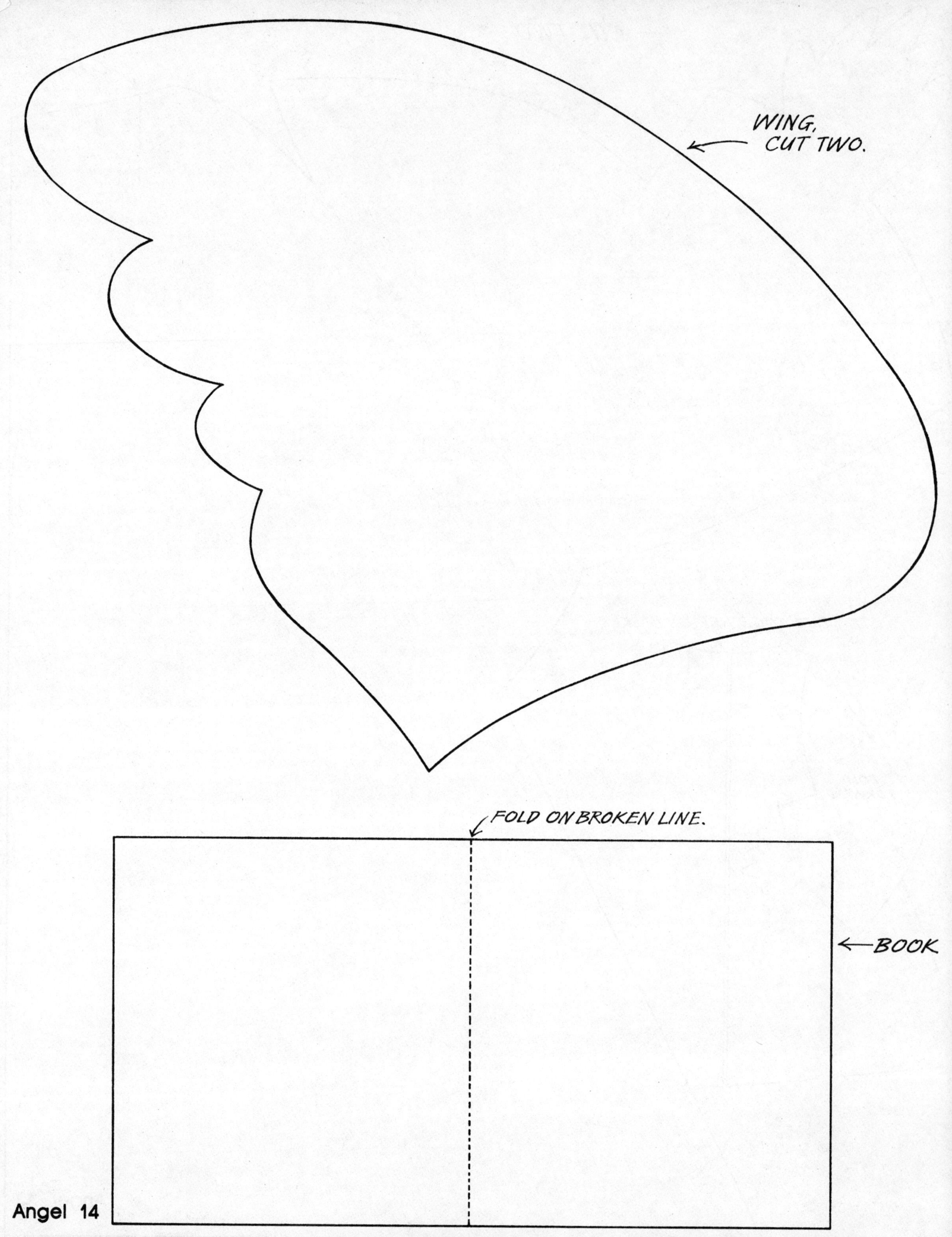

WING,
CUT TWO.
FOLD ON BROKEN LINE.
BOOK
Angel 14

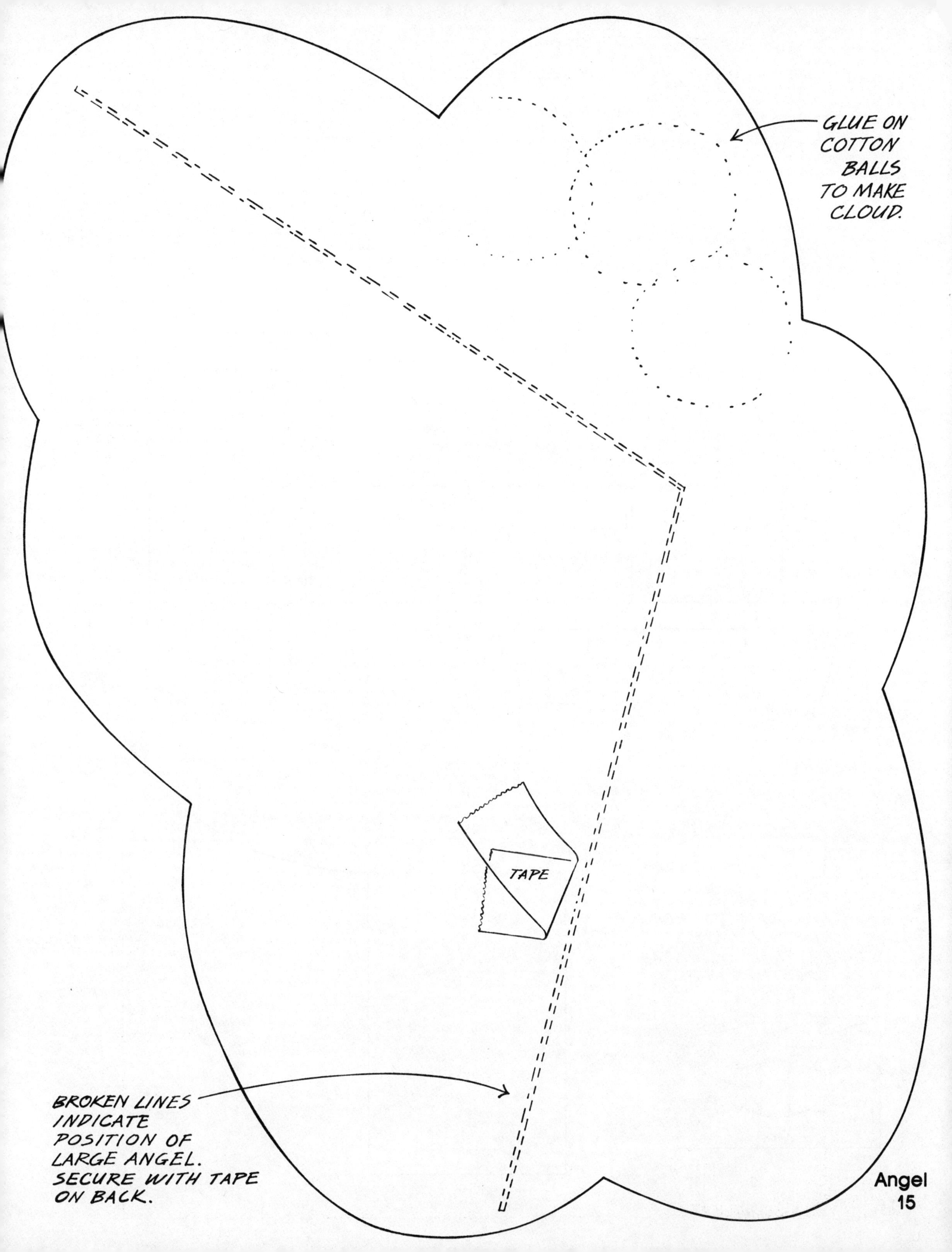

GLUE ON COTTON BALLS TO MAKE CLOUD.
TAPE
BROKEN LINES INDICATE POSITION OF LARGE ANGEL. SECURE WITH TAPE ON BACK.
Angel
15

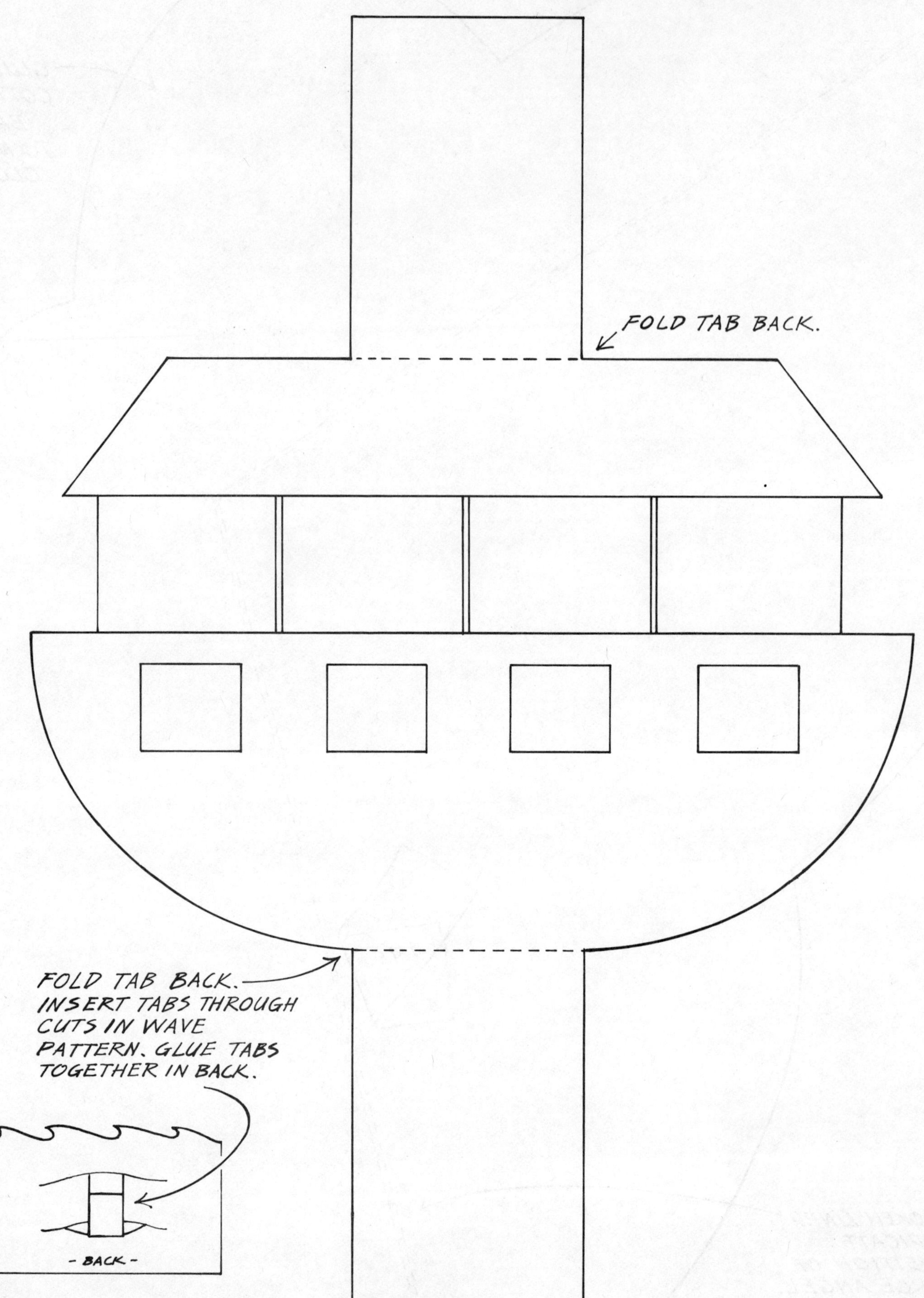

FOLD TAB BACK.
FOLD TAB BACK.
INSERT TABS THROUGH
CUTS IN WAVE
PATTERN. GLUE TABS
TOGETHER IN BACK.
- BACK -

Noah's Ark

Let the children make this movable ark after they have read the Bible story of Noah and the ark.

MATERIALS:

construction paper

crayons or colored pencils

scissors

glue

CONSTRUCTION:

1. Reproduce patterns.

2. Cut out patterns.

3. Have the children draw animals and Noah in the ark, then color.

4. Fold ocean pattern in half, then cut along dotted lines.

5. Slide tabs into ocean pattern, then glue tabs together.

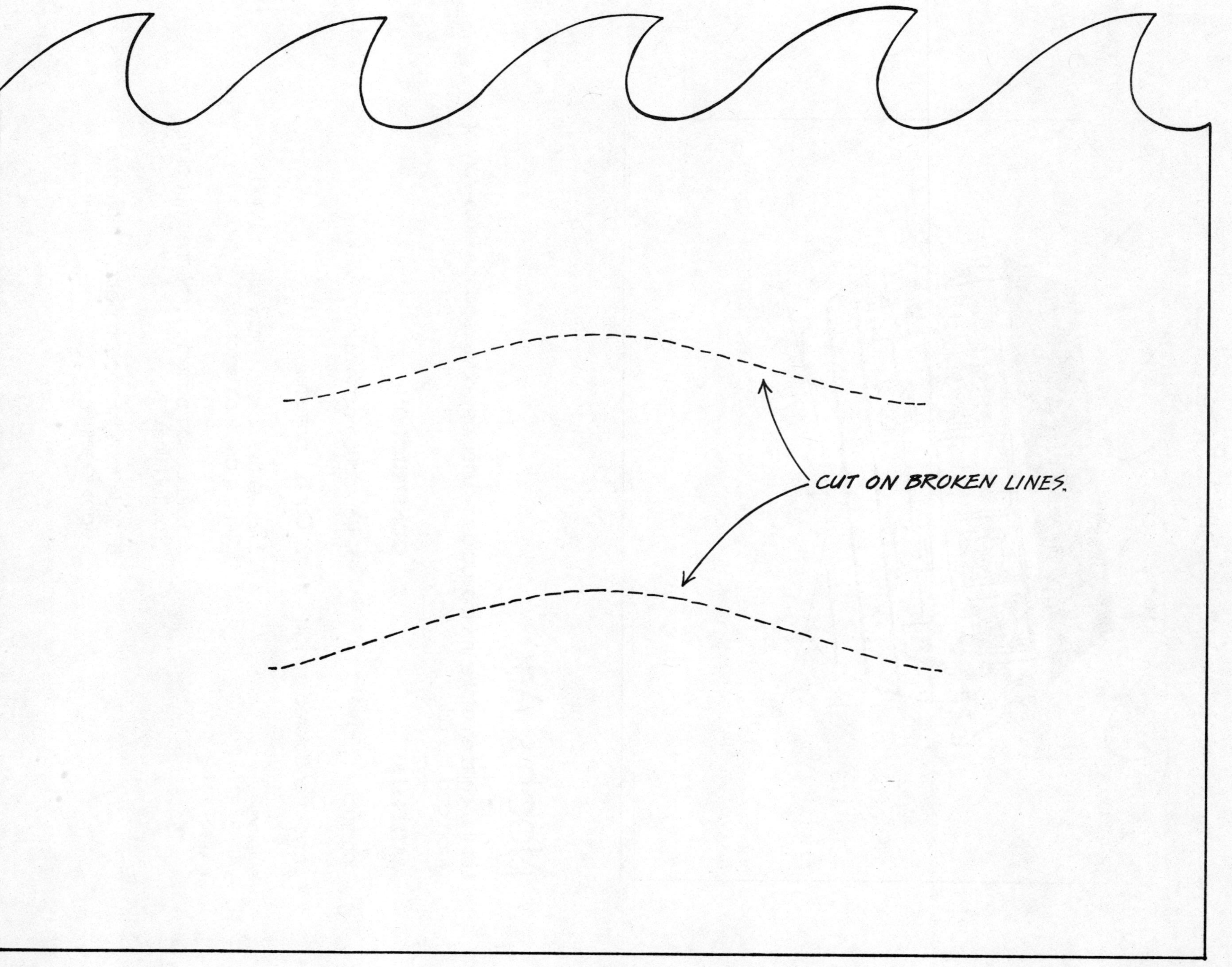

CUT ON BROKEN LINES.

A Gift for Someone Special

Here is a gift idea the children will enjoy giving to someone special.

MATERIALS:

construction paper

12" green pipe cleaners

package of flower seeds
for each child

scissors

glue

crayons

tape

CONSTRUCTION

1. Reproduce patterns.

2. Color and cut out.

3. Glue the flower to the pipe cleaner.

4. Glue the leaves to the pipe cleaner.

5. Tape the flower seed package to the bottom of the pipe cleaner.

6. Place glue around the outer edge of the flower pot. (Do not place glue across the top.) Fold pot over and press edges together.

7. Slide flower seed package down into the flower pot.

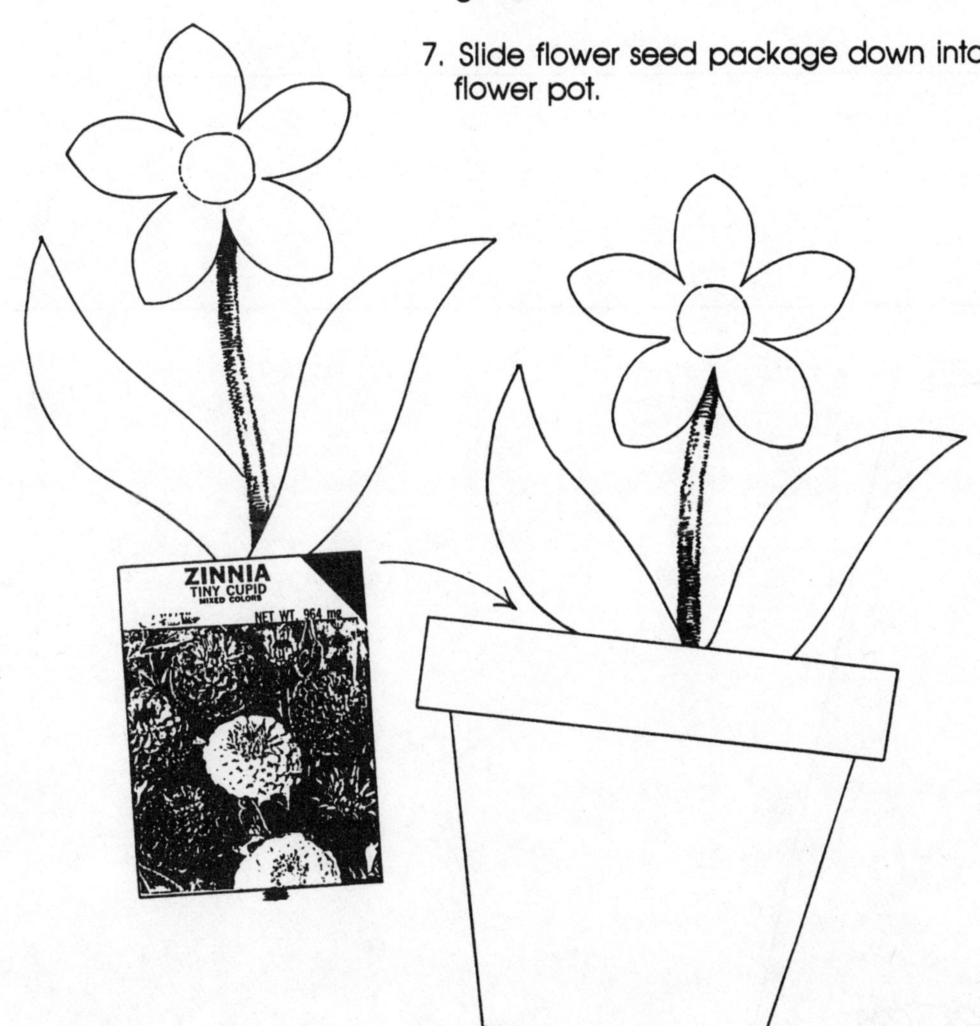

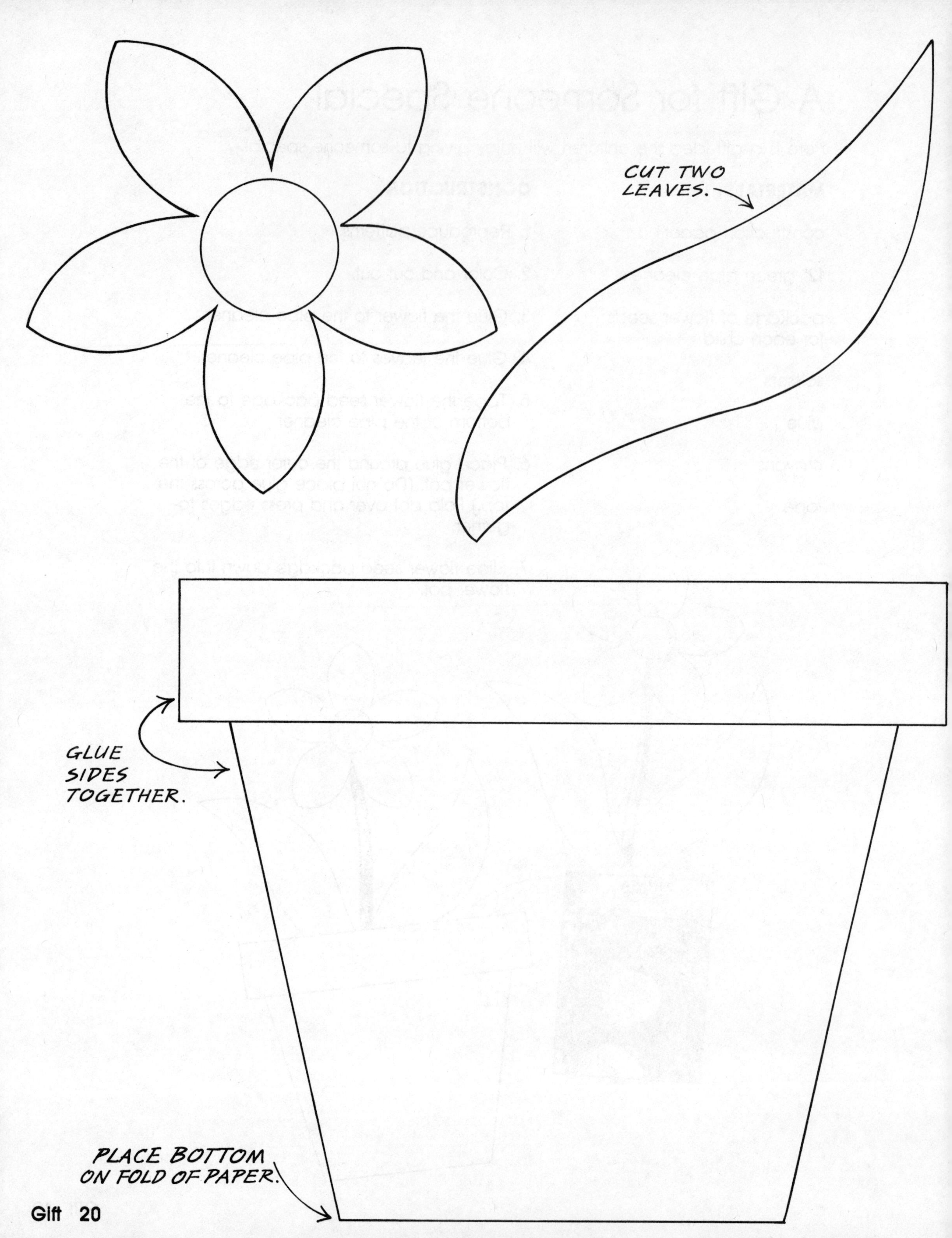

CUT TWO LEAVES.
GLUE SIDES TOGETHER.
PLACE BOTTOM ON FOLD OF PAPER.

God's Rainbow 

This three-dimensional rainbow picture can be made after reading Noah and
the ark. Discuss how God promised never to flood the earth again. God sent
the rainbow as a sign of his promise. A Bible verse can also be written under
the rainbow.

MATERIALS:

construction paper

cotton balls

crayons

scissors

glue

CONSTRUCTION:

1. Reproduce patterns.

2. Color and cut out.

3. Glue cotton balls to clouds.

4. Glue rainbow and clouds to a piece of
   blue construction paper.

5. Cut sun along dotted lines.

6. Fold slit over as shown on pattern and
   glue. This will create a three-dimensional
   sun.

7. Glue sun over rainbow.

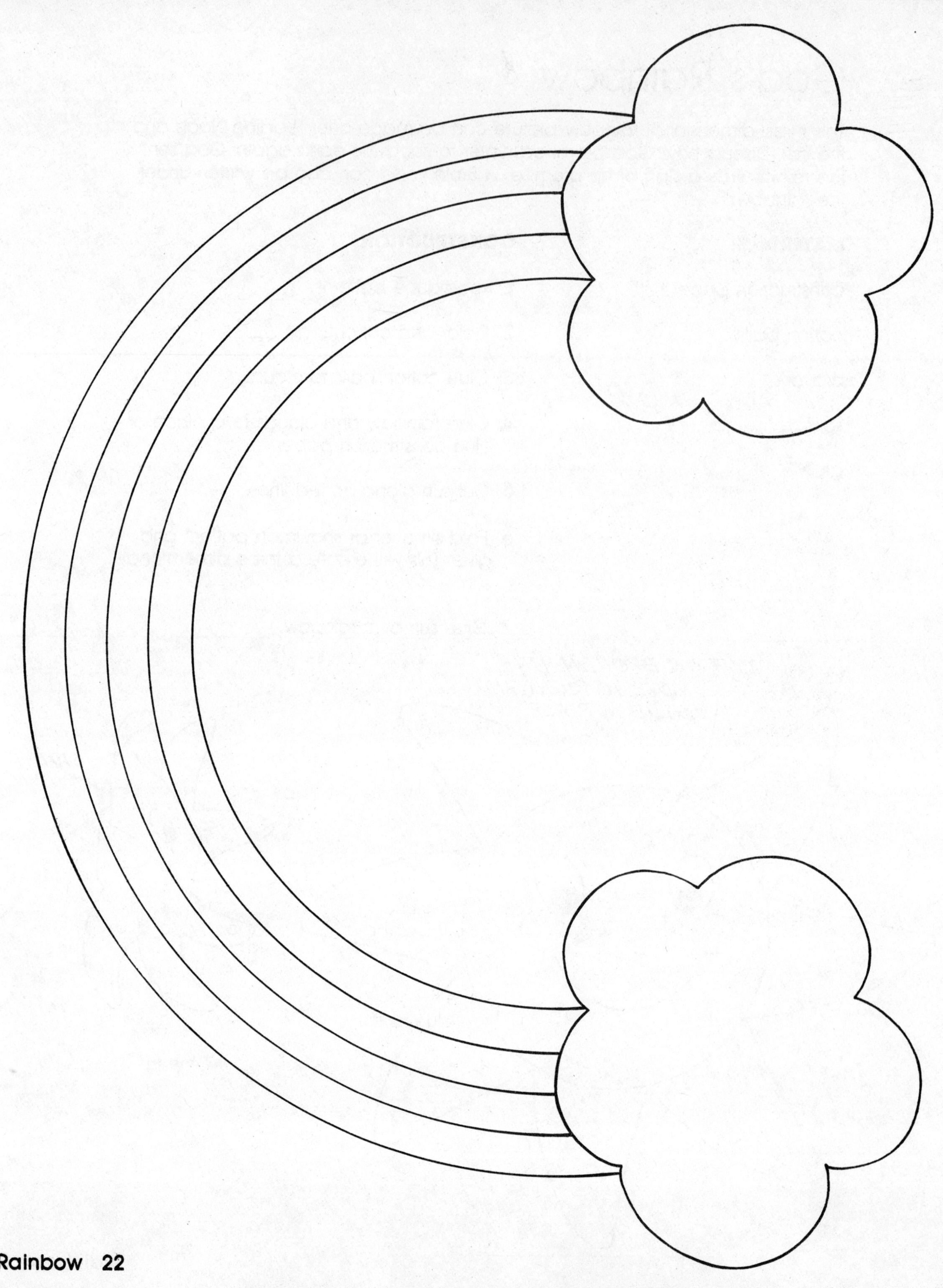

Friendly Frog

Friendly frog is jumping for joy because it is time for Vacation Bible School. This activity can also be used to announce a special church event or program.

MATERIALS:

construction paper

crayons or colored pencils

scissors

glue

CONSTRUCTION:

1. Reproduce patterns.

2. Color and cut out.

3. Cut frog along dotted lines.

4. Fold slits under as shown on pattern and glue. This will create a three-dimensional frog.

5. Place glue on frog as shown on pattern, then glue to the head pattern.

6. Glue foot pattern to the body of the frog.

7. Write a Bible verse or other information on the log.

8. Place frog on log.

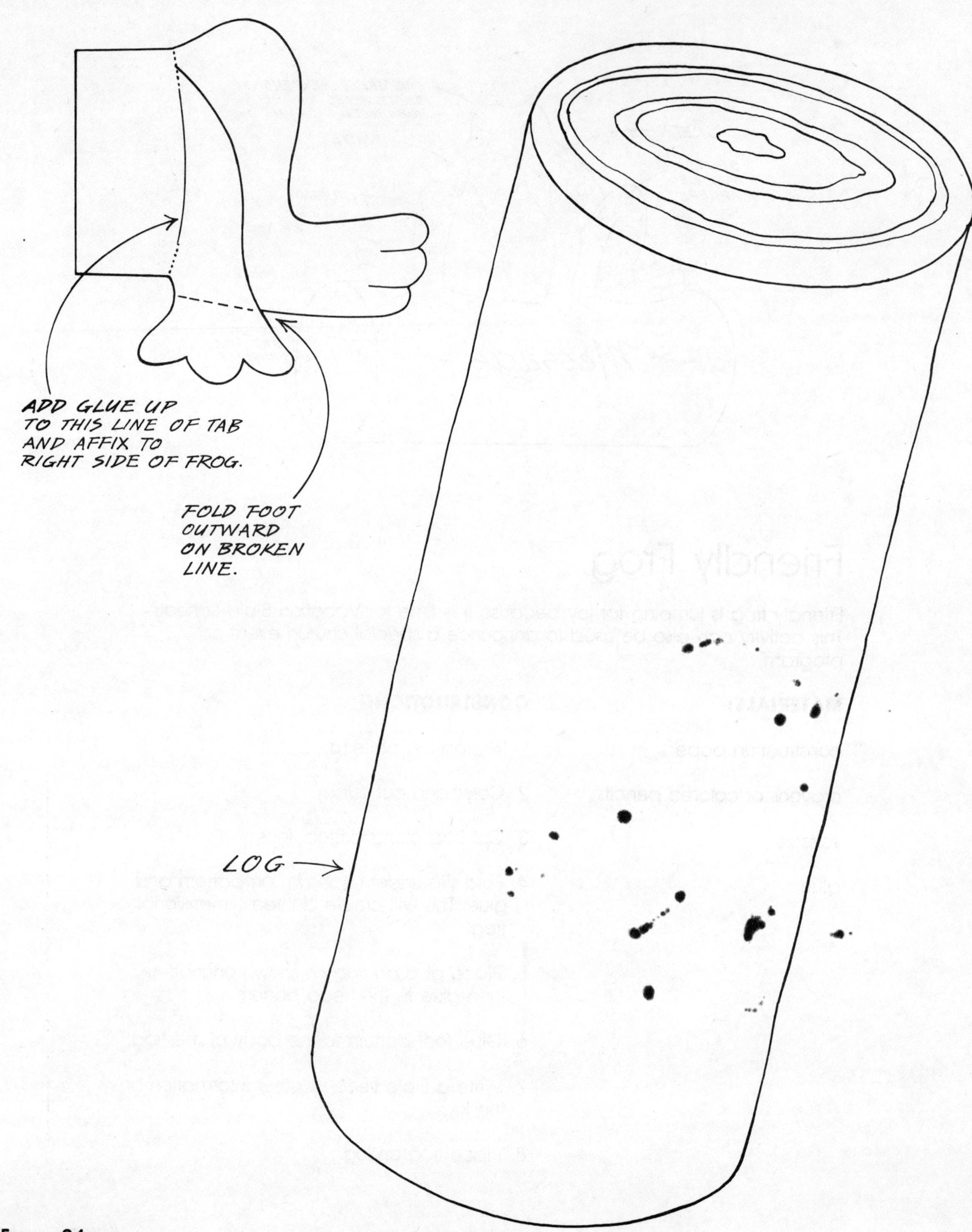

ADD GLUE UP
TO THIS LINE OF TAB
AND AFFIX TO
RIGHT SIDE OF FROG.
FOLD FOOT
OUTWARD
ON BROKEN
LINE.
LOG →

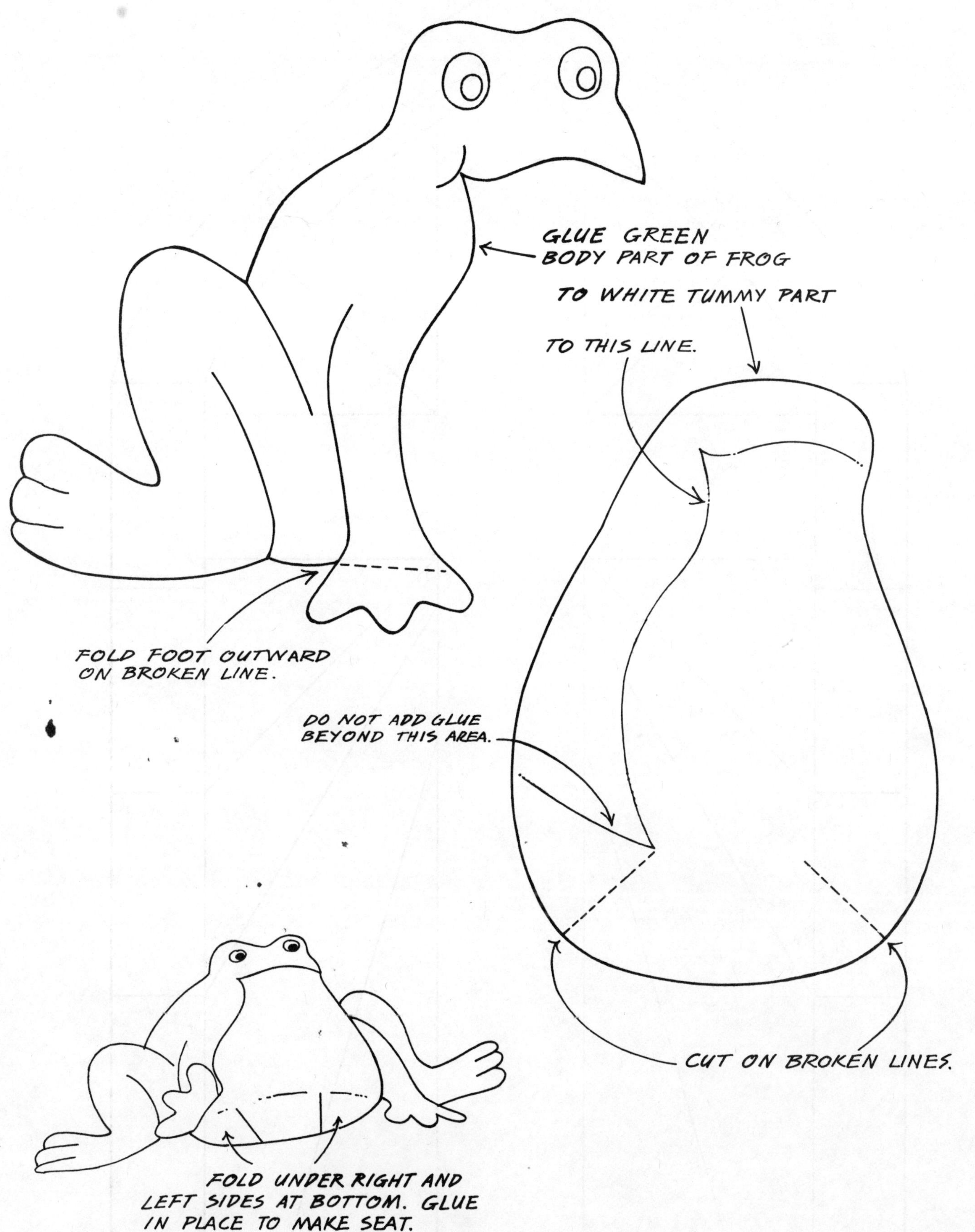

GLUE GREEN BODY PART OF FROG TO WHITE TUMMY PART TO THIS LINE.
FOLD FOOT OUTWARD ON BROKEN LINE.
DO NOT ADD GLUE BEYOND THIS AREA.
CUT ON BROKEN LINES.
FOLD UNDER RIGHT AND LEFT SIDES AT BOTTOM. GLUE IN PLACE TO MAKE SEAT.

Window 26

Stained-glass Window

Everyone will enjoy designing a colorful stained-glass window.

MATERIALS:

lightweight cardboard

plastic wrap or colored cellophane

crayons or colored pencils

tape

CONSTRUCTION:

1. Reproduce pattern.

2. Trace pattern onto a piece of lightweight cardboard, color, and cut out.

3. Cover finished window with plastic wrap or colored cellophane. Tape in place on back.

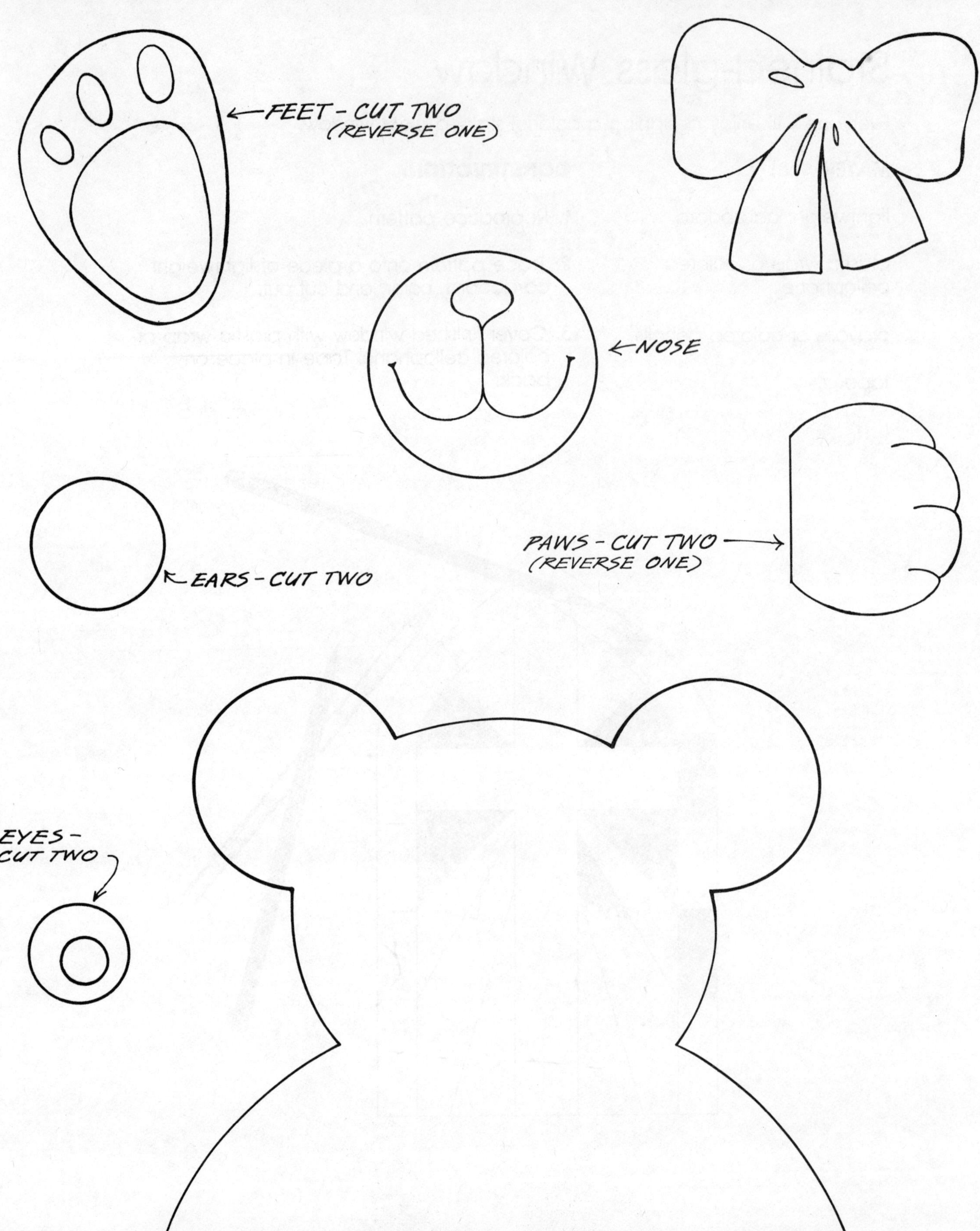

FEET - CUT TWO
(REVERSE ONE)
NOSE
EARS - CUT TWO
PAWS - CUT TWO
(REVERSE ONE)
EYES -
CUT TWO

Share Bear Sack

The share bear sack is a fun way to share something special with the Sunday school or Vacation Bible School class.

MATERIALS:

construction paper

lunch sacks

crayons

scissors

glue

CONSTRUCTION:

1. Reproduce pattern.

2. Cut out pattern.

3. Place bear's head pattern on top of sack, trace around it, and cut out.

4. Open sack up, fold sides down, and cut off.

5. Draw and color features on the bear or cut features out of construction paper, then glue to sack.

ADD GLUE TO TOP
OF HEAD AND AFFIX
TO TOP PIECE OF
SHELL.
DESIGNS ARE OPTIONAL.
CHILDREN MAY WANT TO
CREATE THEIR OWN.

Chick

This charming pop-up chick can be used as an Easter card to wish someone a happy Easter or used as an Easter egg hunt invitation. Write the information for the hunt on the chick.

MATERIALS:

construction paper

crayons

scissors

glue

CONSTRUCTION:

1. Reproduce patterns.

2. Color and cut out.

3. Cut egg pattern along dotted lines.

4. Glue top of egg to the chick's head. Glue bottom of egg to a piece of construction paper.

5. Slide chick into egg.

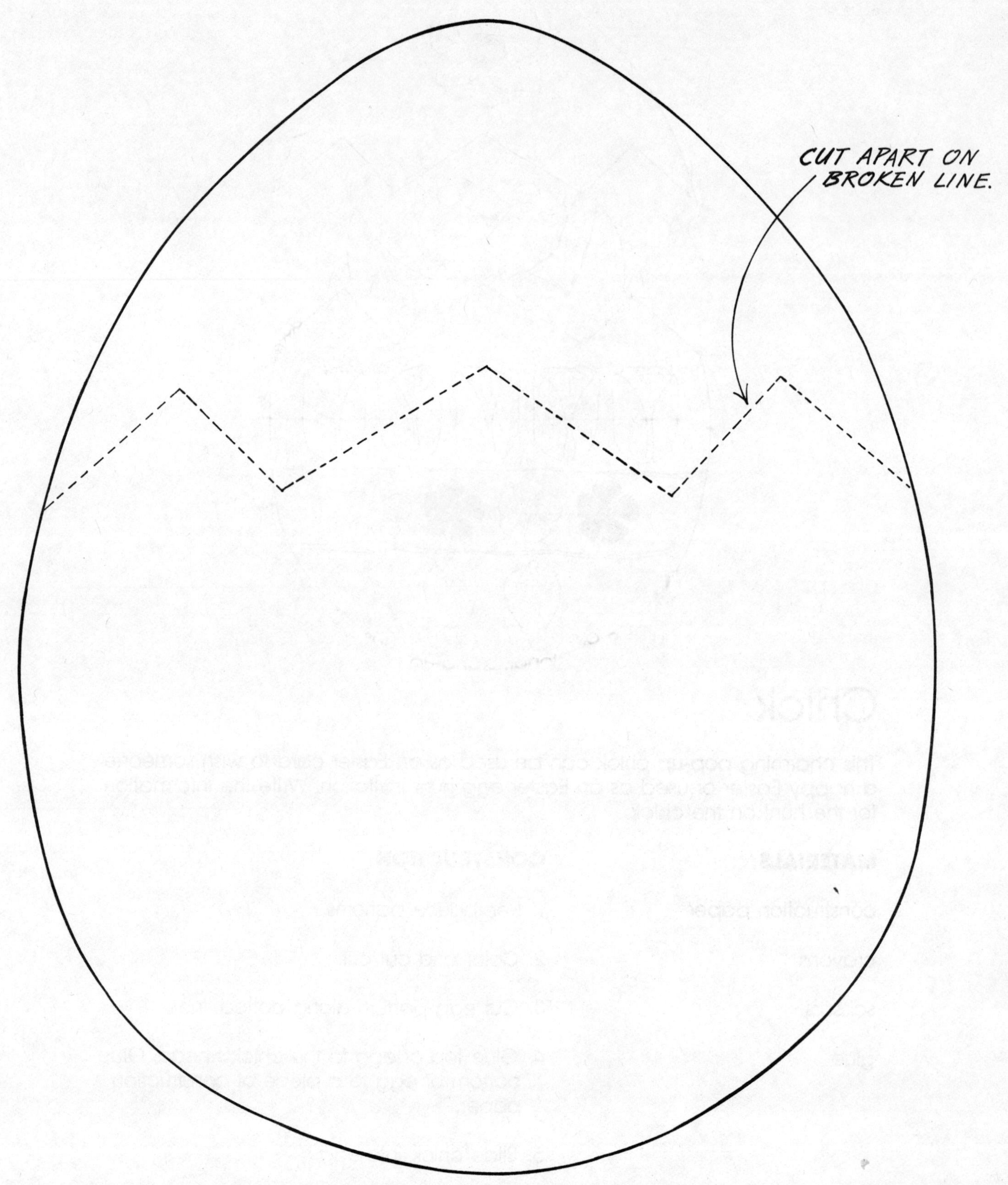

CUT APART ON
BROKEN LINE.

The Creation

Talk to the class about the creation of the heavens and the earth. Let the children make this three-dimensional, stand-up picture.

MATERIALS:

construction paper

crayons or colored pencils

scissors

CONSTRUCTION:

1. Reproduce patterns onto construction paper.

2. Cut out the half circle, then draw and color God's creation.

3. Color and cut out the trees.

4. Cut along dotted lines of trees and the half circle. Slot trees and half circle together.

5. Stand picture up for display.

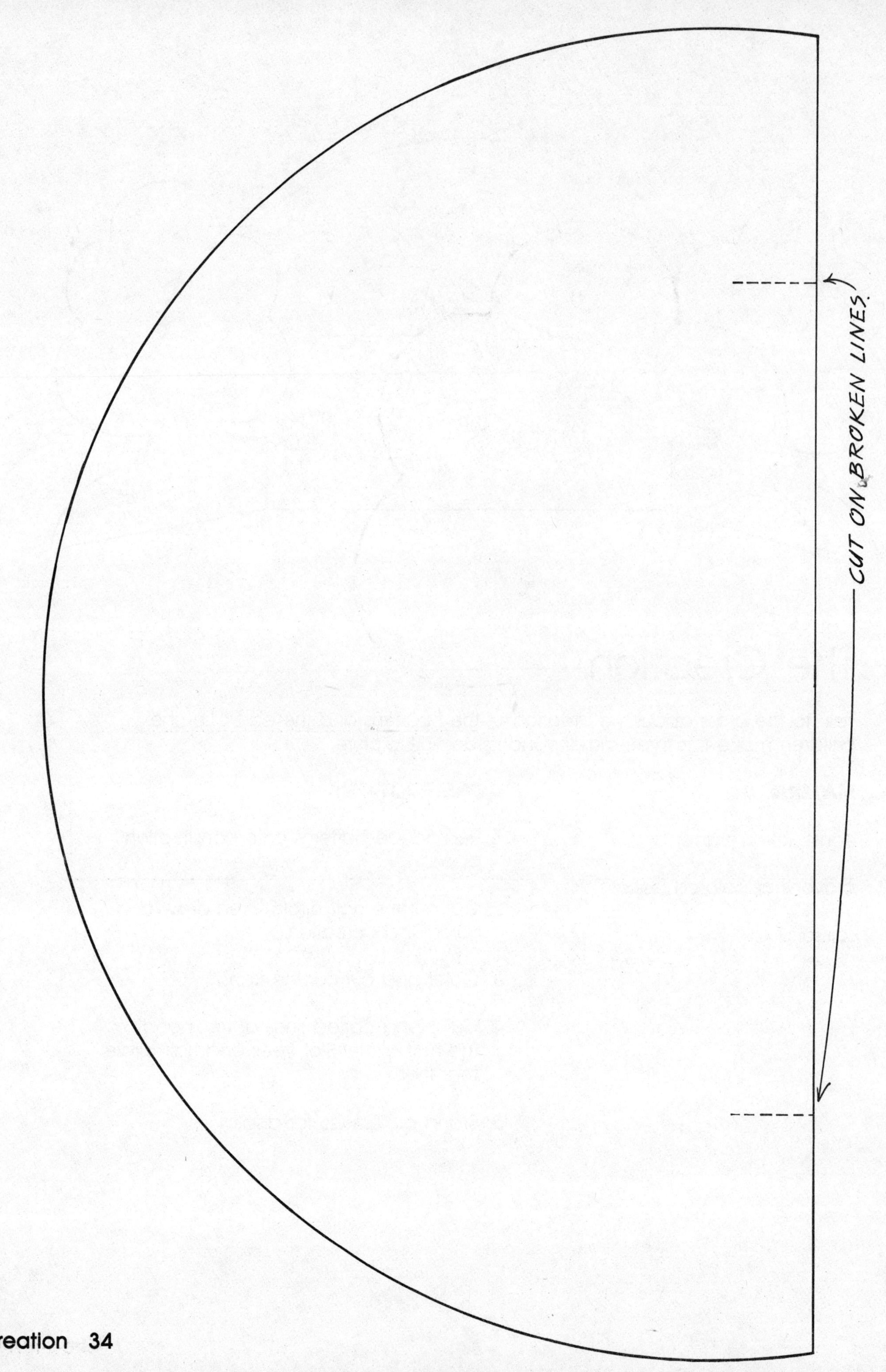

CUT ON BROKEN LINES.

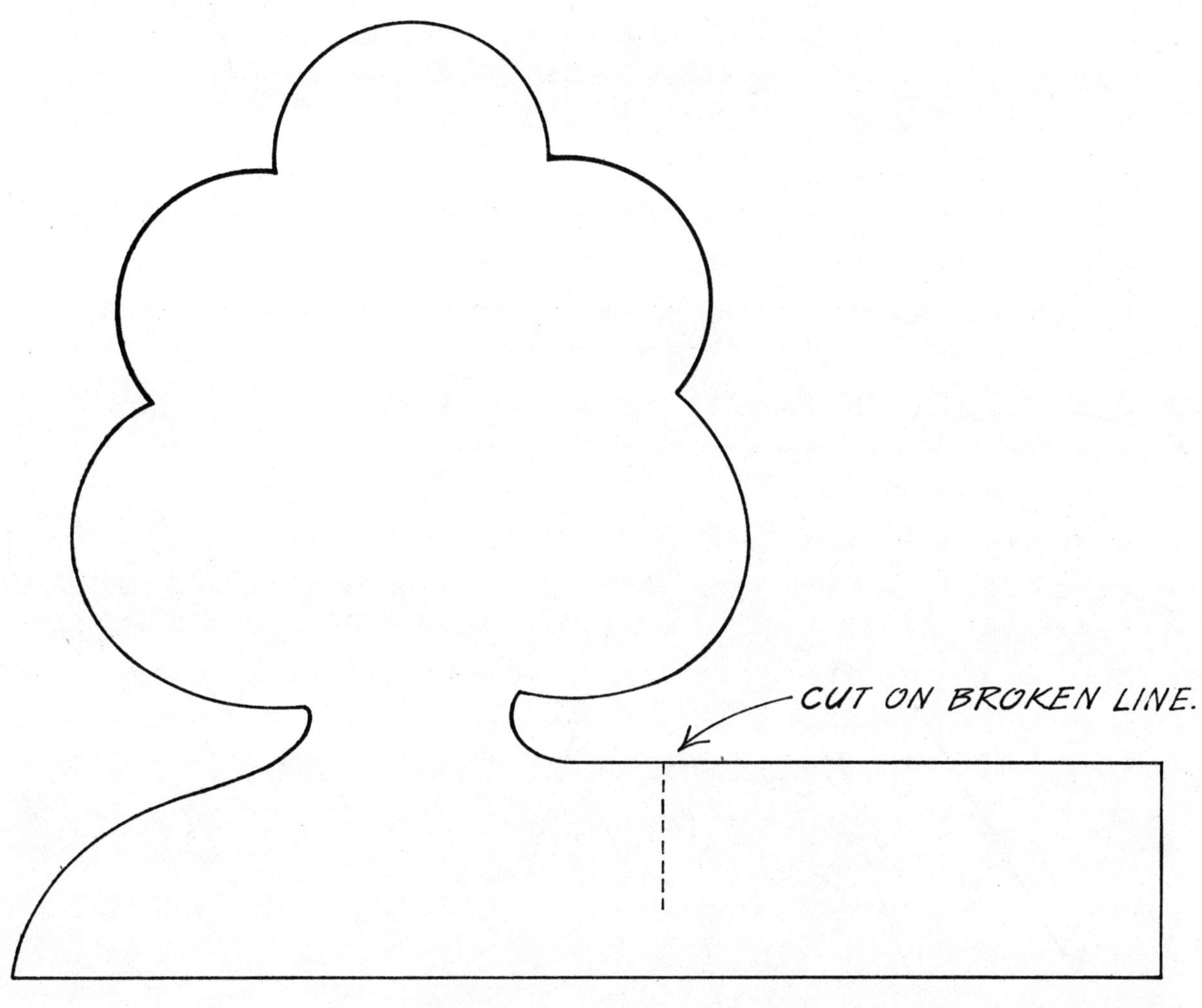

CUT ON BROKEN LINE.
CUT TWO – REVERSE ONE.

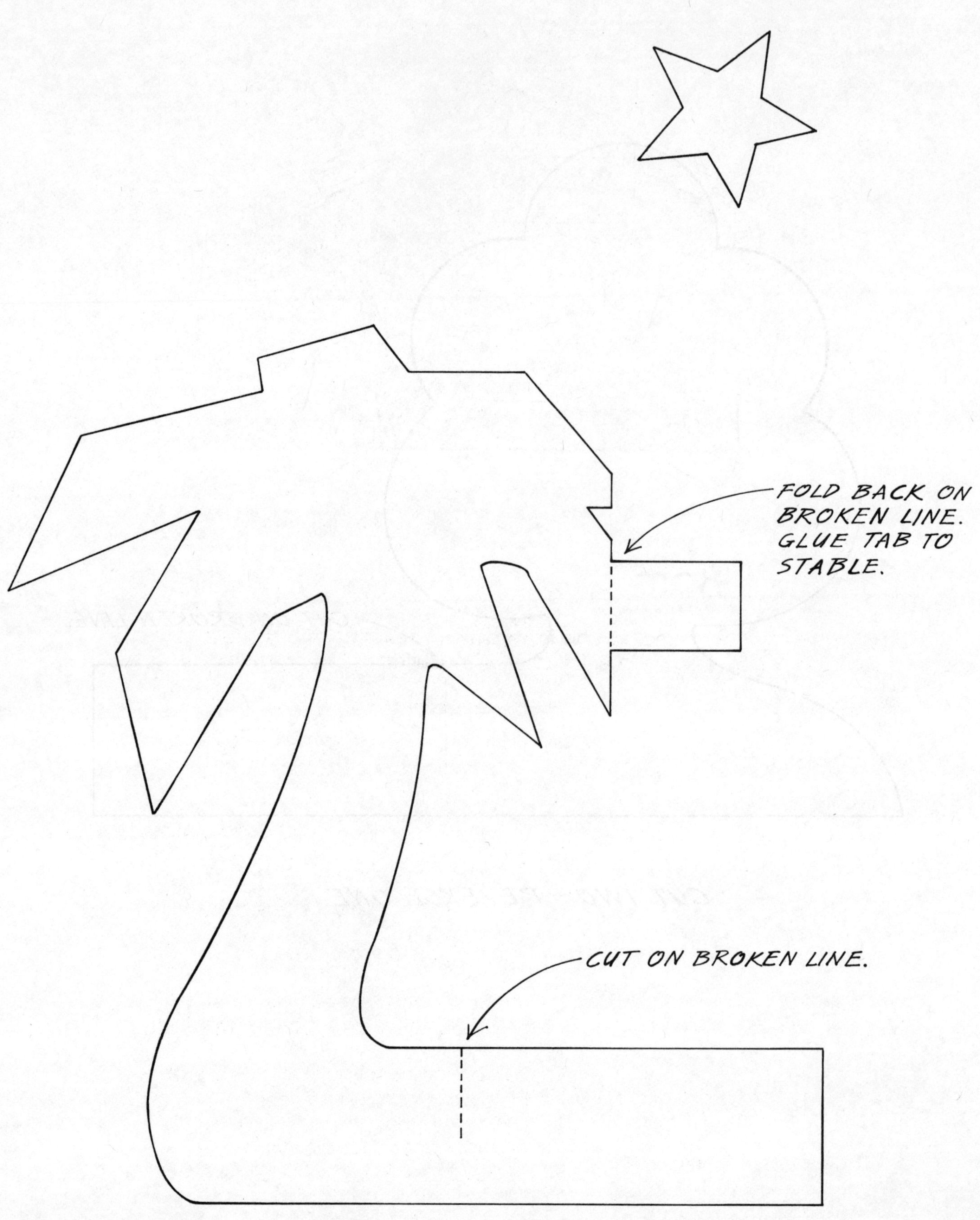
FOLD BACK ON
BROKEN LINE.
GLUE TAB TO
STABLE.
CUT ON BROKEN LINE.

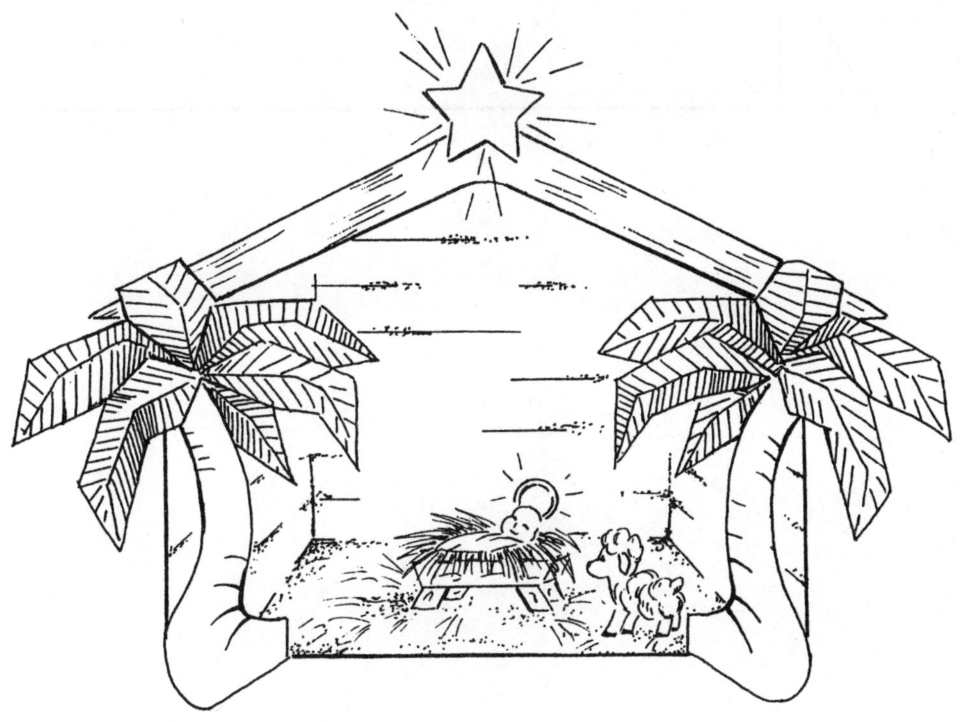

Christ Is Born

The children will enjoy making this three-dimensional, stand-up manger scene. This makes a nice display to enjoy during the Christmas season.

MATERIALS:

construction paper

crayons or colored pencils

scissors

glue

CONSTRUCTION:

1. Reproduce patterns onto construction paper.

2. Cut out manger, then draw and color the manger scene.

3. Glue the star to the top of the manger.

4. Color and cut out two trees.

5. Cut along dotted lines of the trees and the manger. Slot trees and manger together.

6. Fold tree tabs back, place glue on tabs, then glue to manger.

7. Stand manger up for display.

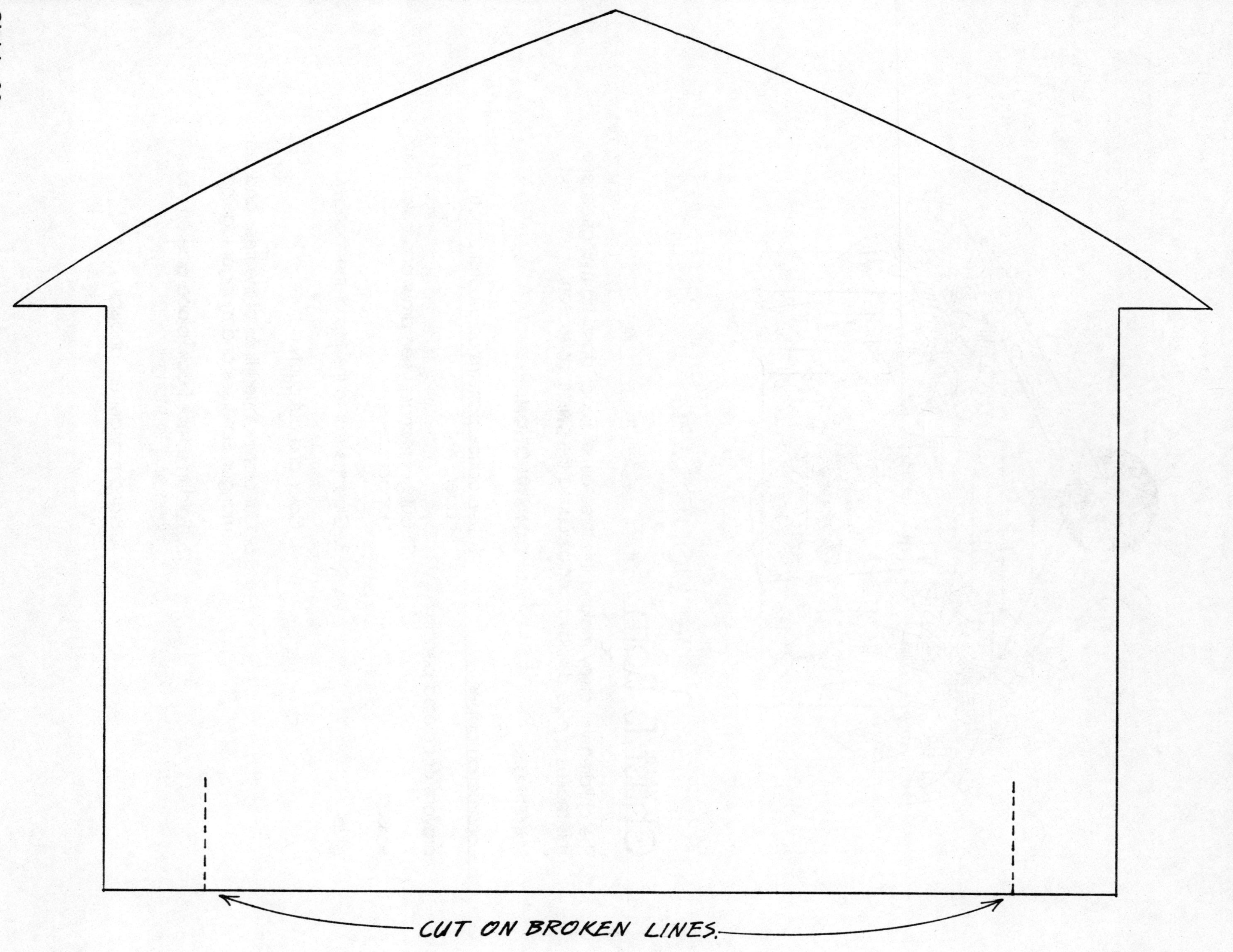

CUT ON BROKEN LINES.

Daniel in the Lion's Den

Read the Bible story of Daniel in the lion's den, then let the children create this stand-up Daniel and lion.

MATERIALS:

construction paper

crayons or color pencils

scissors

glue

CONSTRUCTION:

1. Reproduce patterns.

2. Color and cut out.

3. Overlap the two sides of the pattern of Daniel, then glue.

4. Glue the head on.

5. Overlap the two sides of the lion pattern, then glue.

6. Cut slits around the circle, then curl slits out with pencil. This will be the lion's mane.

7. Glue head to mane, then glue to the lion's body.

8. Glue tail on.

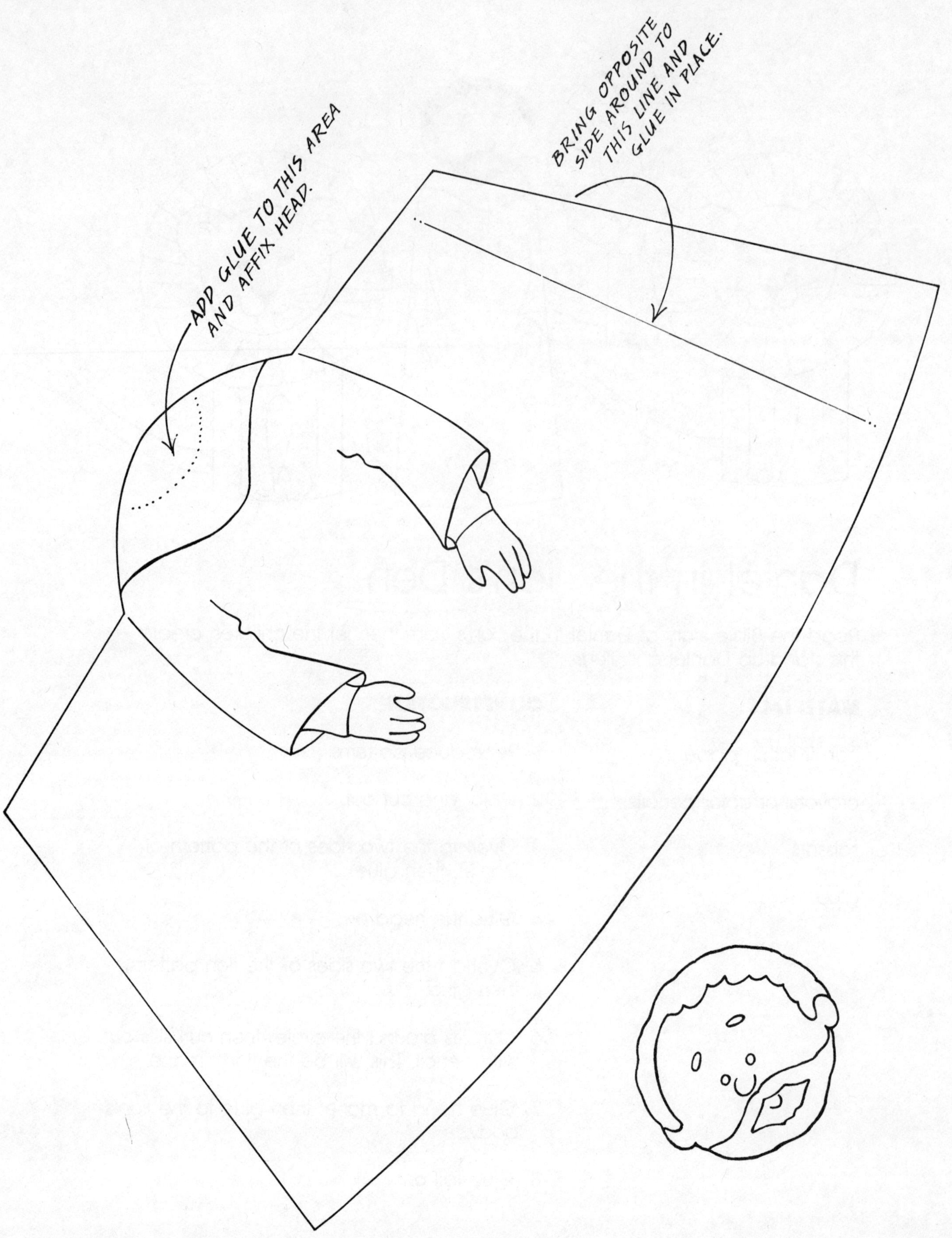

ADD GLUE TO THIS AREA AND AFFIX HEAD.
BRING OPPOSITE SIDE AROUND TO THIS LINE AND GLUE IN PLACE.

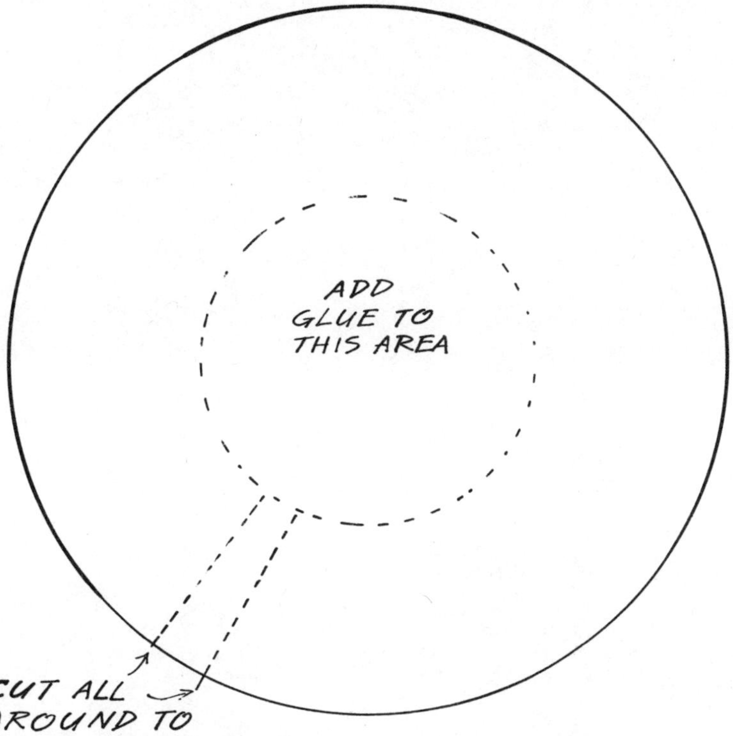

CUT ALL
AROUND TO
BROKEN CENTER
LINE AND CURL OUTWARD.

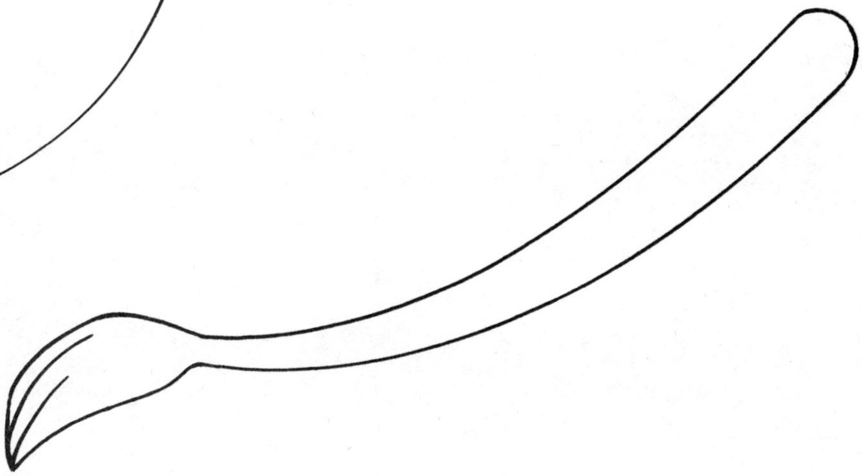

BRING OPPOSITE SIDE
AROUND TO THIS LINE
AND GLUE IN PLACE.

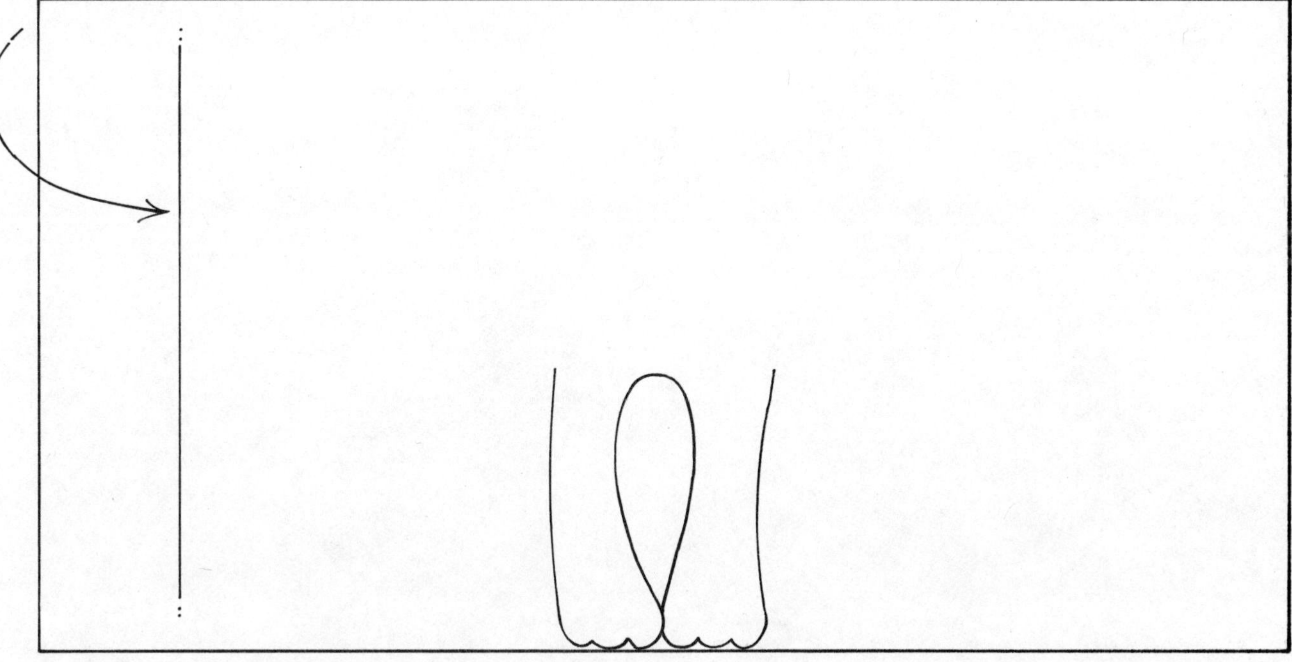

CUT ON BROKEN LINE.

Jonah and the Whale

Read the story of Jonah and the whale. Let the children make this three-dimensional whale.

MATERIALS:

construction paper

crayons

scissors

glue

CONSTRUCTION:

1. Reproduce pattern.

2. Color and cut out.

3. Cut whale along dotted lines.

4. Fold slit over as shown on pattern and glue. This will create a three-dimensional whale.

5. Curl tail out with pencil.

6. Place glue on back of whale, then glue to construction paper.

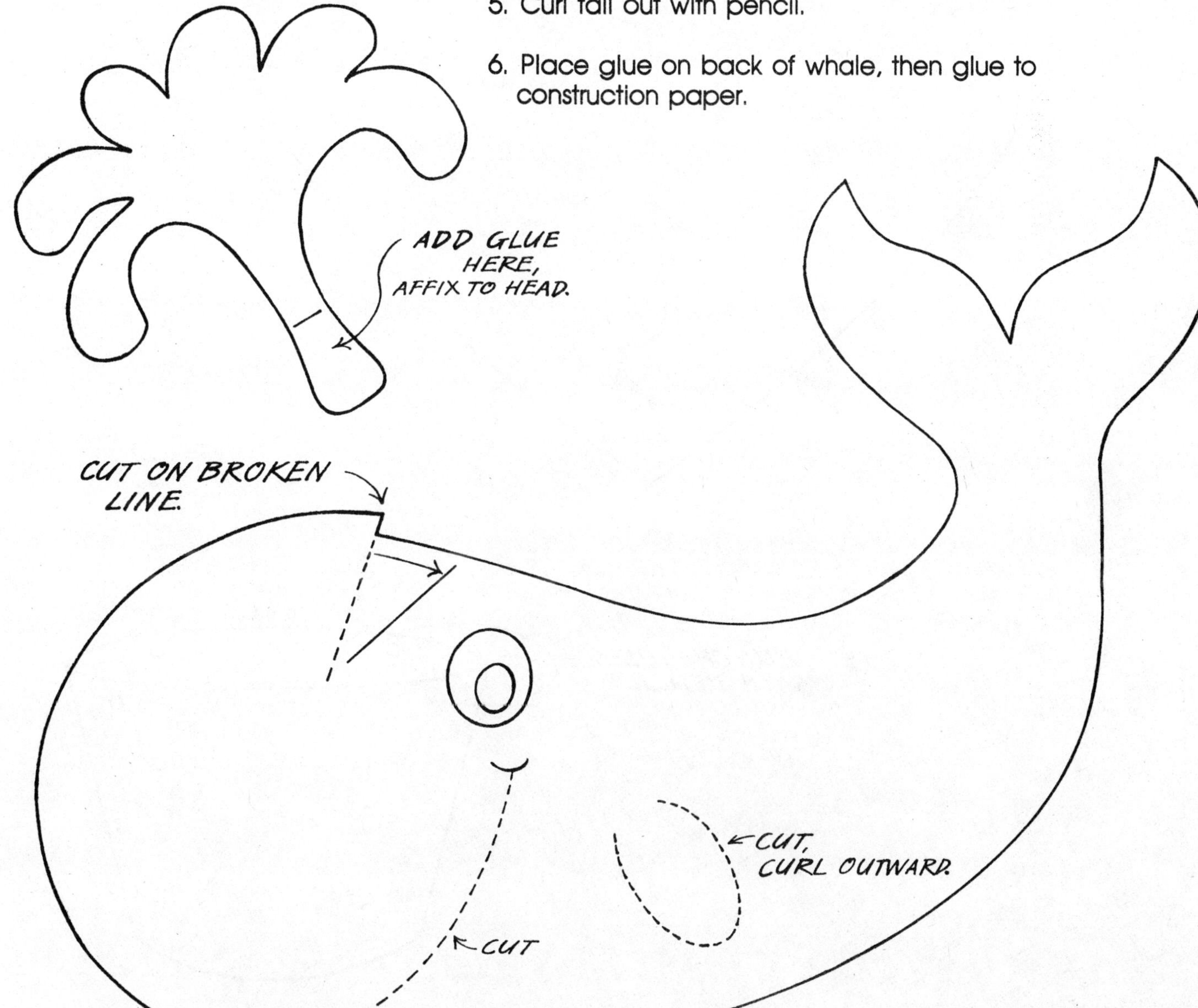

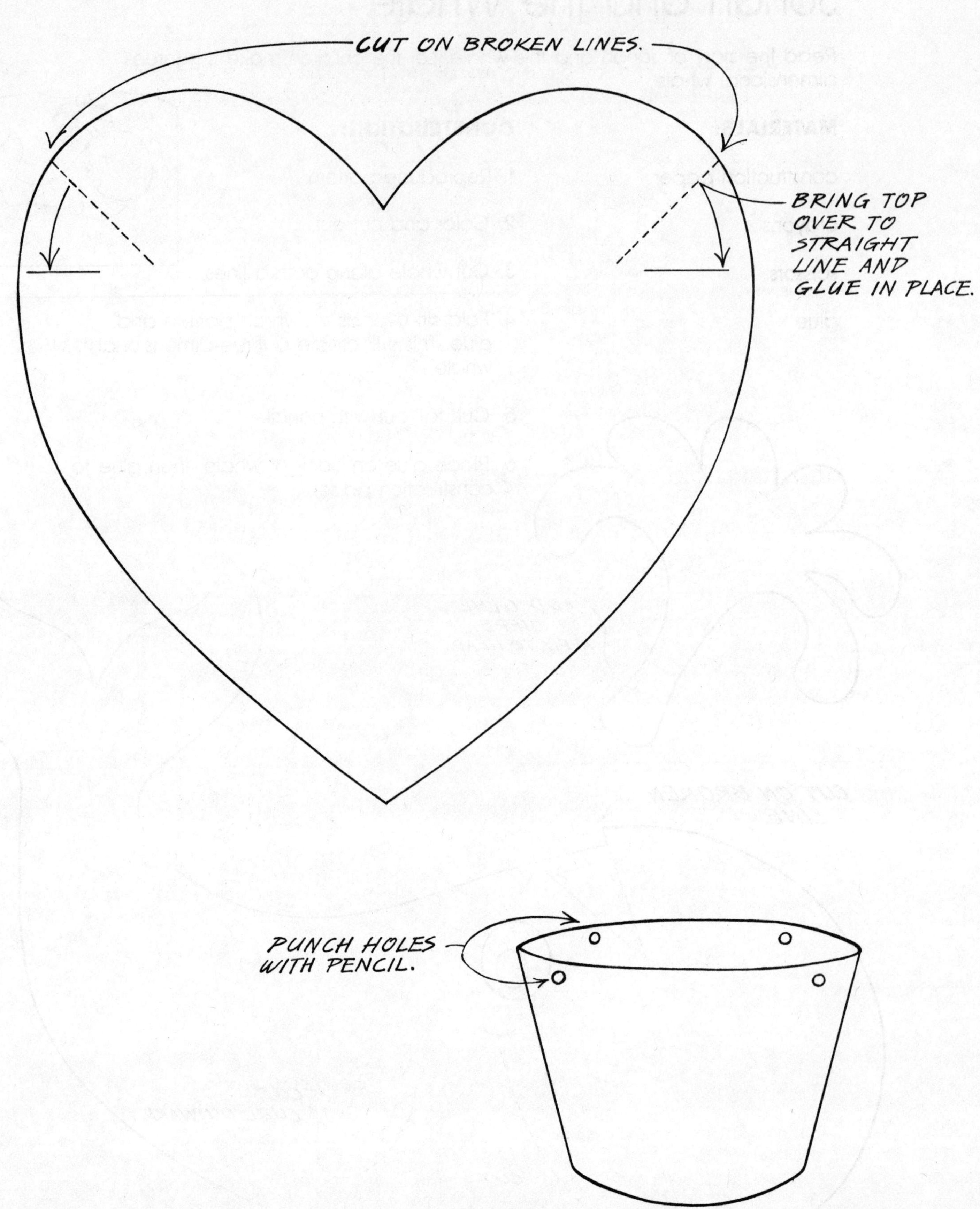

CUT ON BROKEN LINES.
BRING TOP OVER TO STRAIGHT LINE AND GLUE IN PLACE.
PUNCH HOLES WITH PENCIL.

Hot Air Balloon

Up, up, and away in a three-dimensional heart air balloon. The balloons can either be glued to a piece of construction paper or attached to a bulletin board for display.

MATERIALS:

construction paper

yarn

crayons

scissors

glue

CONSTRUCTION:

1. Reproduce patterns.

2. Color and cut out.

3. Write a Bible verse on the heart.

4. Have the children draw themselves on a piece of construction paper, color, cut out, and glue to basket.

5. Cut balloon along dotted lines.

6. Fold slits over as shown on pattern and glue. This will create a three-dimensional heart balloon.

7. Attach balloon to basket with yarn.

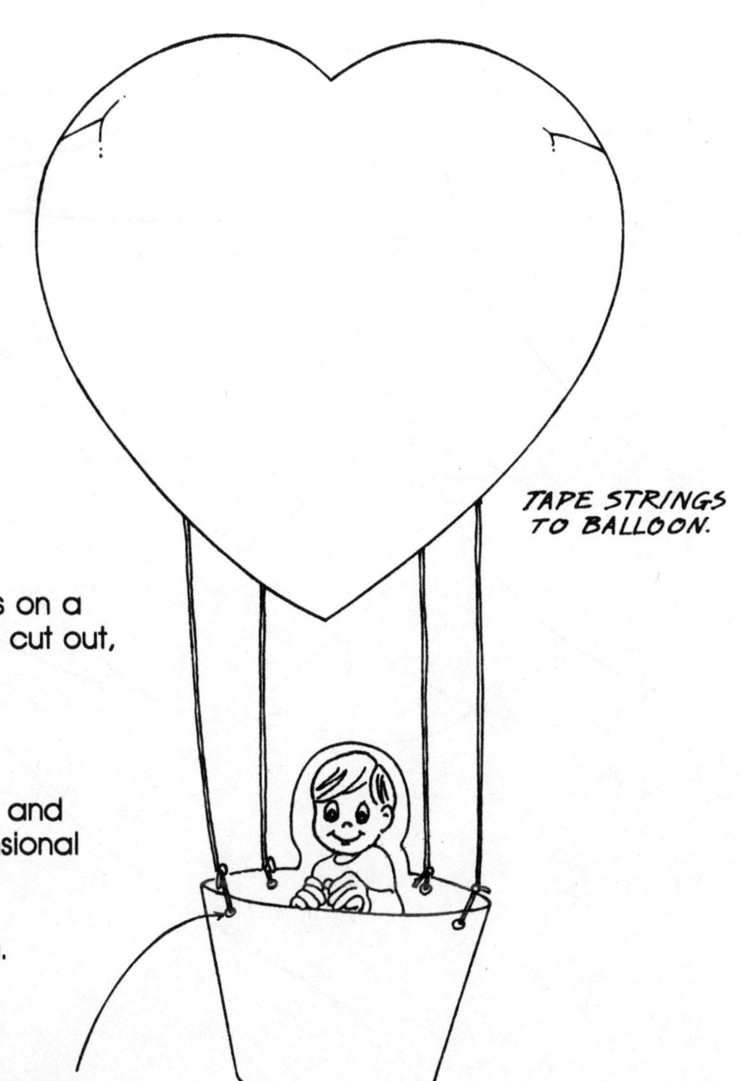

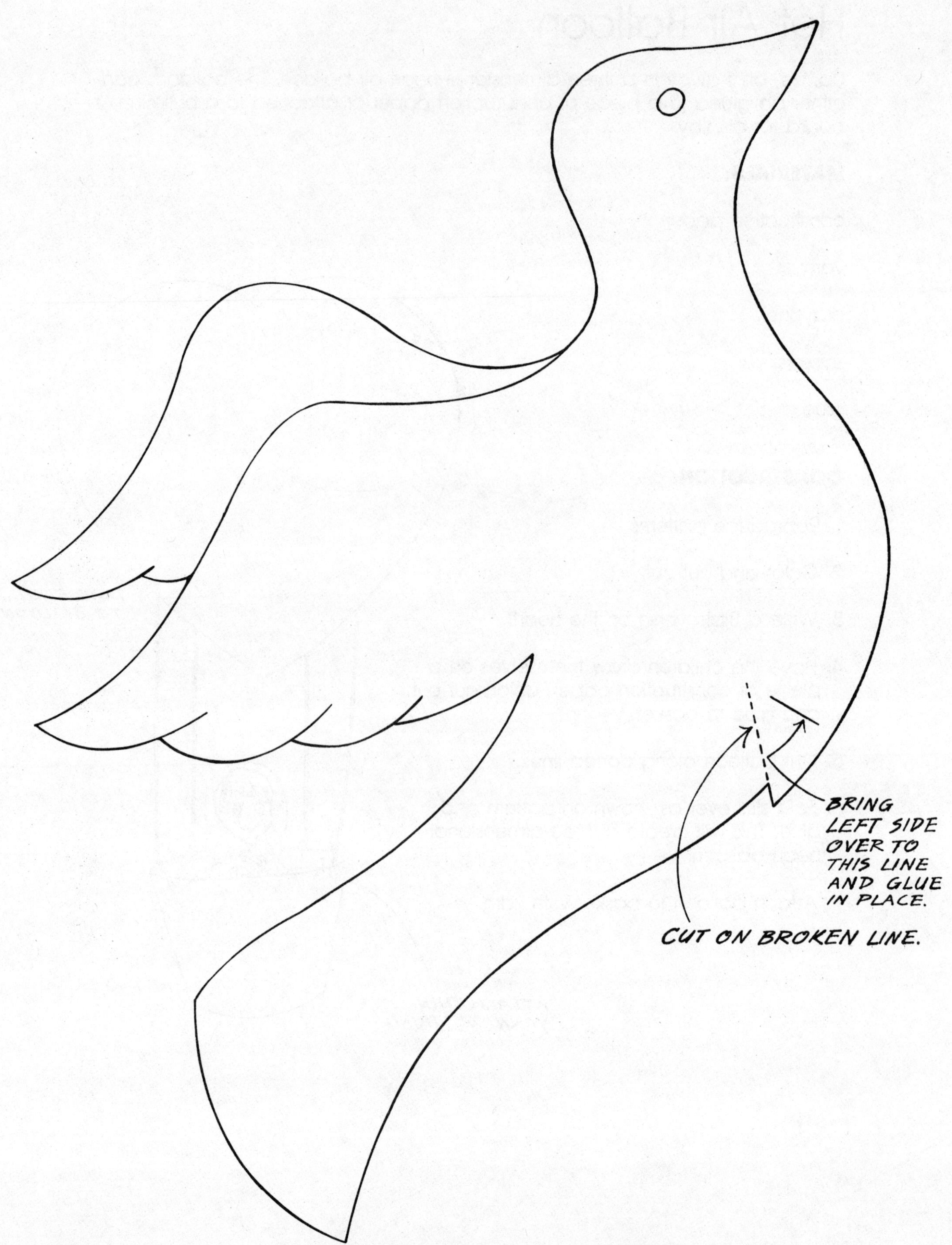

BRING LEFT SIDE OVER TO THIS LINE AND GLUE IN PLACE.
CUT ON BROKEN LINE.

Dove 46

Dove

Let the children make this three-dimensional dove. Have them write a Bible verse on the cloud.

MATERIALS:

construction paper

crayons or colored pencils

scissors

glue

CONSTRUCTION:

1. Reproduce patterns.

2. Color and cut out.

3. Cut along dotted lines.

4. Fold slit over as shown on pattern and glue. This will create a three-dimensional dove.

5. Place glue on the back of the wings, then glue to cloud.

6. Write a Bible verse on the cloud.

←CLOUD

Owl

This stand-up owl is a creative way to reinforce lessons. Write the information being studied on the branch.

MATERIALS:

construction paper

crayons or colored pencils

scissors

glue

CONSTRUCTION:

1. Reproduce patterns.

2. Color and cut out.

3. Cut along dotted lines.

4. Overlap the sides of the owl pattern, then glue.

5. Insert wings into the slits of the body.

6. Glue the head to the body.

7. Write information on branch.

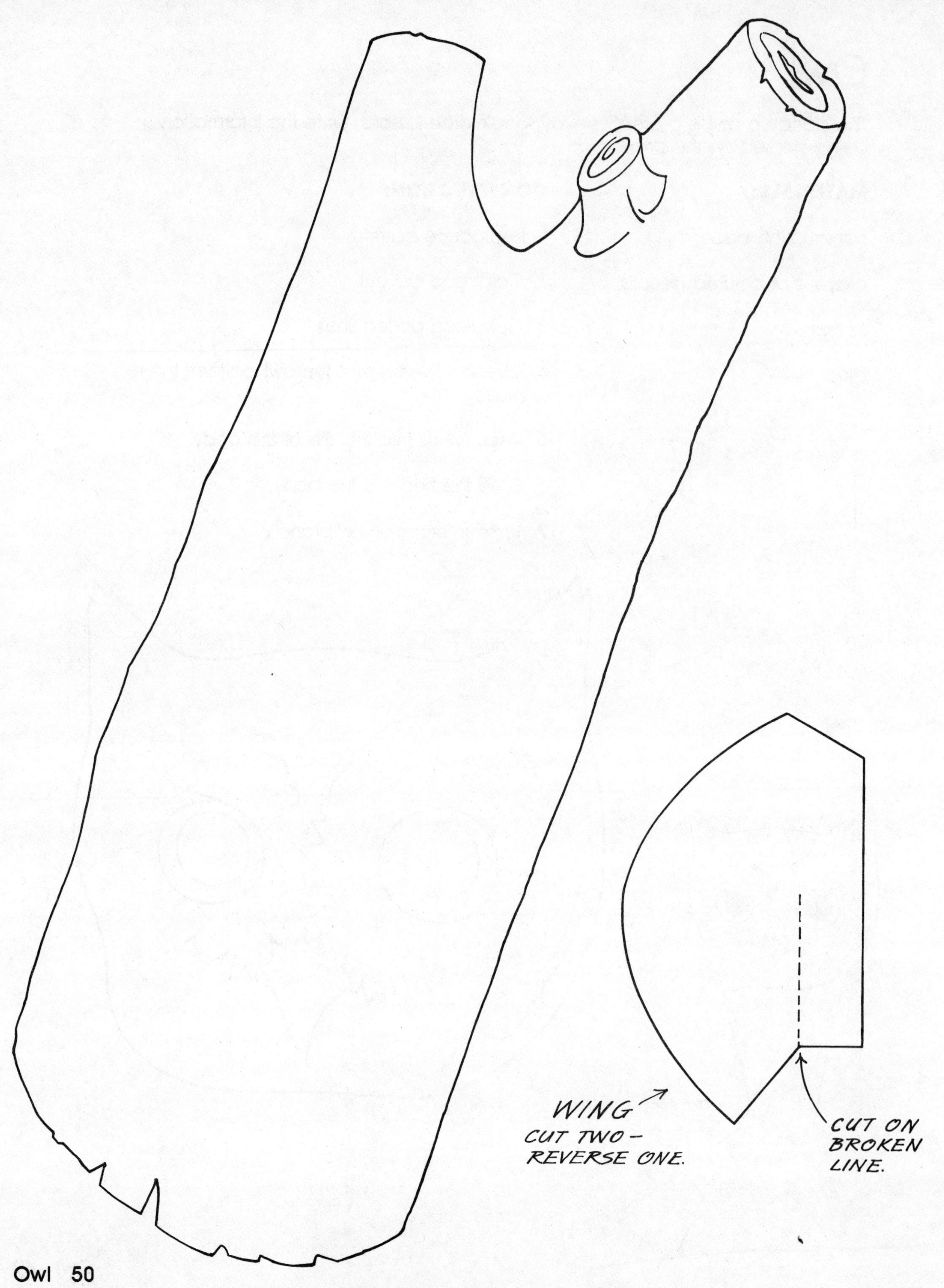

WING
CUT TWO—
REVERSE ONE.
CUT ON
BROKEN
LINE.

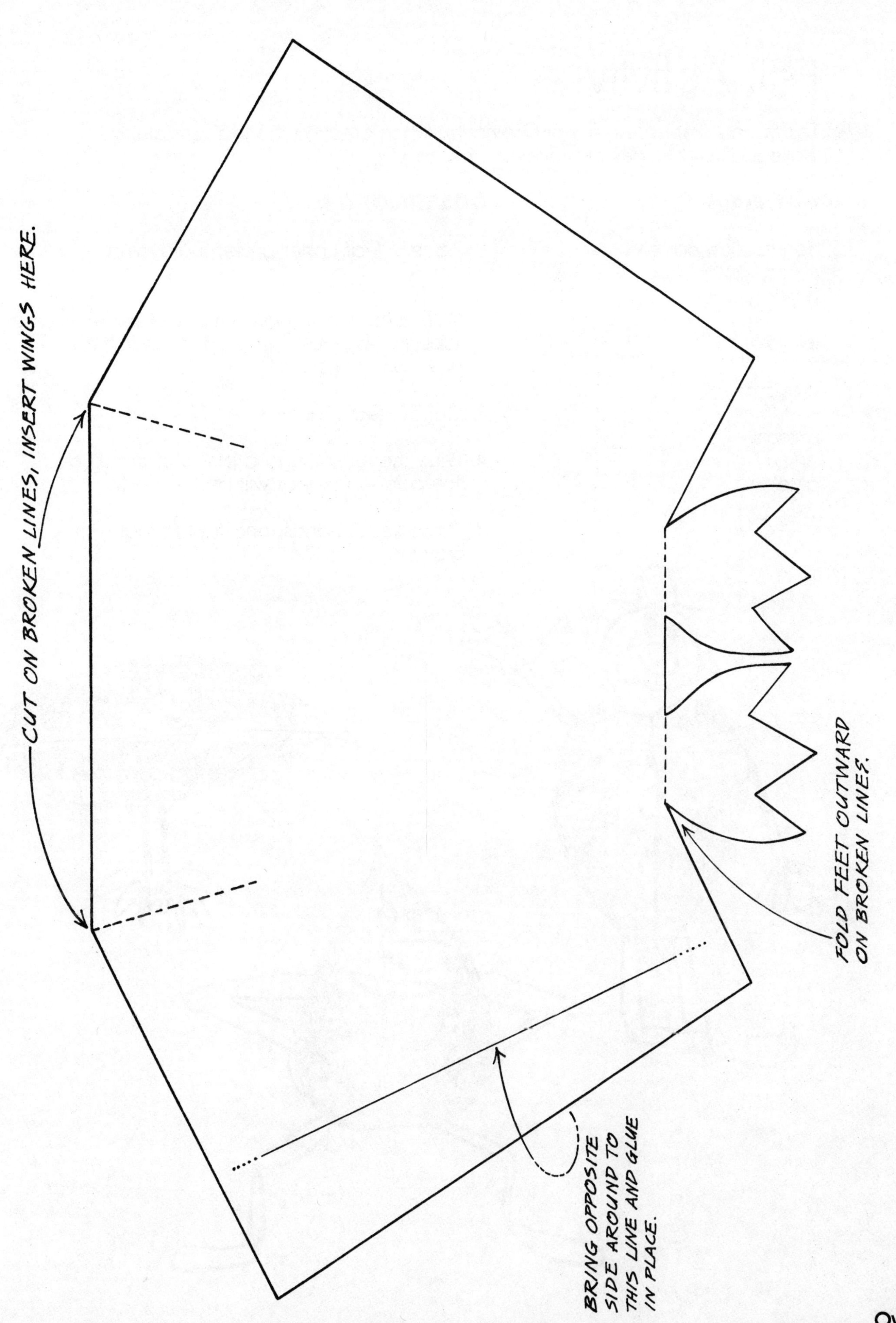

CUT ON BROKEN LINES, INSERT WINGS HERE.
FOLD FEET OUTWARD ON BROKEN LINES.
BRING OPPOSITE SIDE AROUND TO THIS LINE AND GLUE IN PLACE.

Fall Activity

Tell the children to use their imagination when creating the leaf people. Collect different types of leaves for this activity.

MATERIALS:

construction paper

typing paper

leaves

crayons

scissors

glue

CONSTRUCTION:

1. Place a leaf under a piece of typing paper.

2. With a crayon rub the surface of the leaf through the paper, working in the same direction all the time.

3. Cut out leaf rubbings.

4. Glue the rubbings to a piece of construction paper. The leaf will be the body.

5. Draw head, hands, and feet to leaf with crayons.

Snowman

This three-dimensional crystal glitter snowman will brighten up a cold winter's day.

MATERIALS:

construction paper

crystal glitter

crayons

scissors

glue

CONSTRUCTION:

1. Reproduce patterns.

2. Color and cut out.

3. Cut along dotted lines.

4. Fold slits over as shown on pattern. This will create a three-dimensional snowman.

5. Spread glue over the snowman, then sprinkle with crystal glitter.

6. Place glue on the back of the snowman's head, then glue to a piece of construction paper.

7. Accessories can be cut out of construction paper and glued to the snowman.

8. Color a snow scene around the snowman.

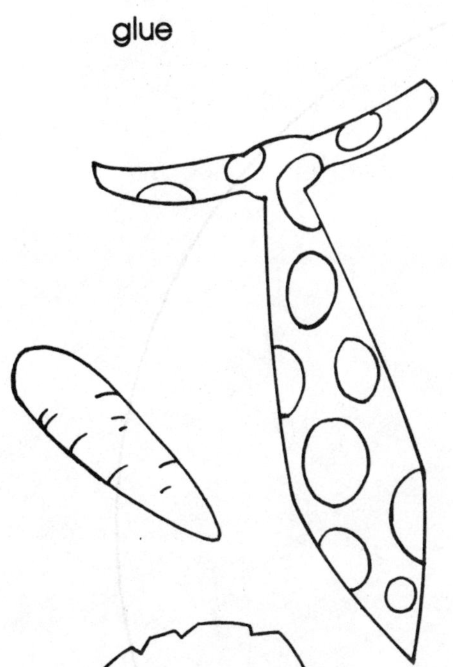

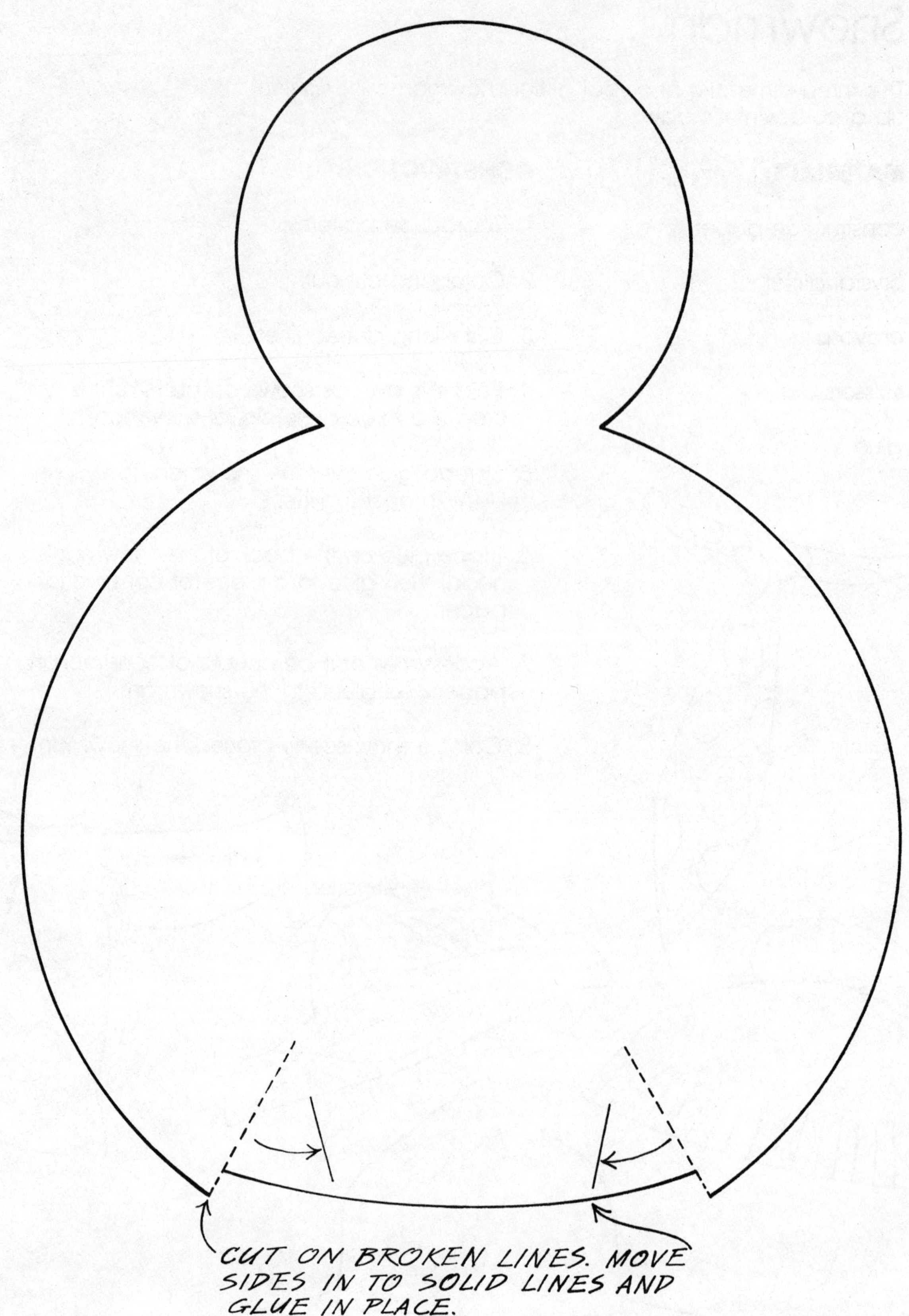

CUT ON BROKEN LINES. MOVE
SIDES IN TO SOLID LINES AND
GLUE IN PLACE.

Spring Activity

Celebrate the season with a colorful spring basket filled with flowers.

MATERIALS:

construction paper

crayons

scissors

glue

CONSTRUCTION:

1. Reproduce patterns.

2. Cut out basket, then cut along dotted lines.

3. Trace and cut out four strips with the pattern provided. Use a contrasting color for the strips.

4. Weave each strip over and under through the basket.

5. Trim each strip and glue to the basket.

6. Glue the basket to a piece of construction paper.

7. Draw spring flowers in the basket, then color. Flowers can also be cut out of colored construction paper, then glued to the basket.

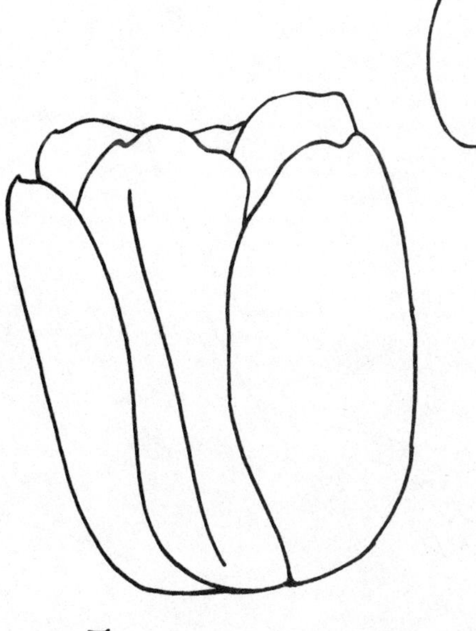

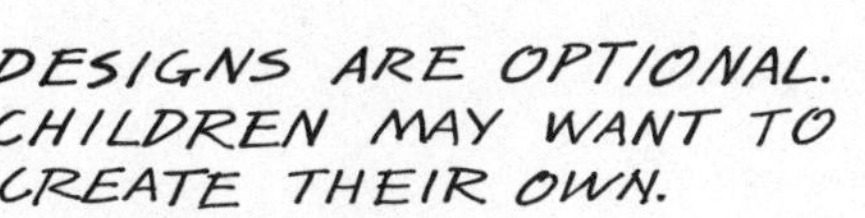

CUT FOUR
CUT ON BROKEN LINES.

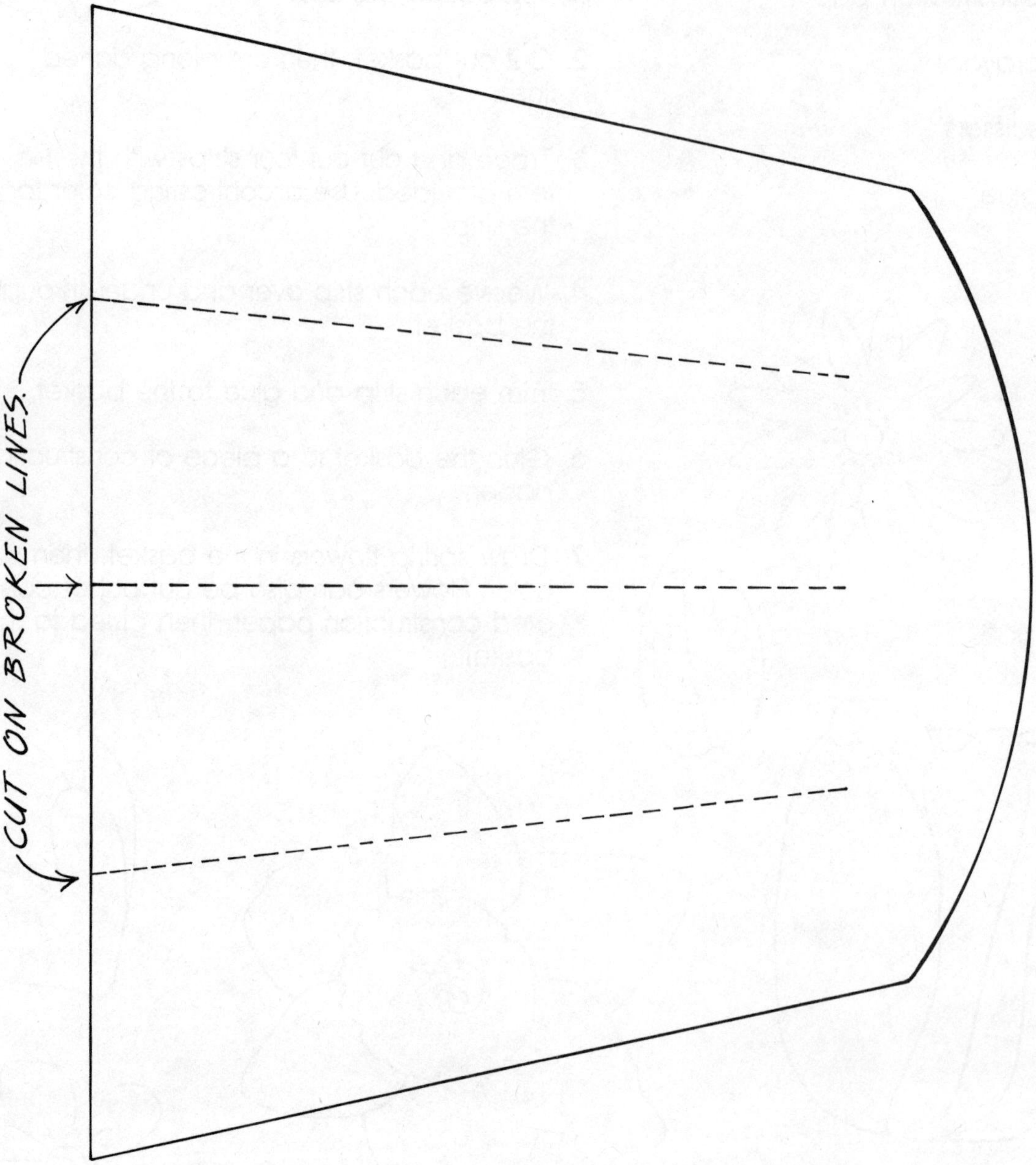

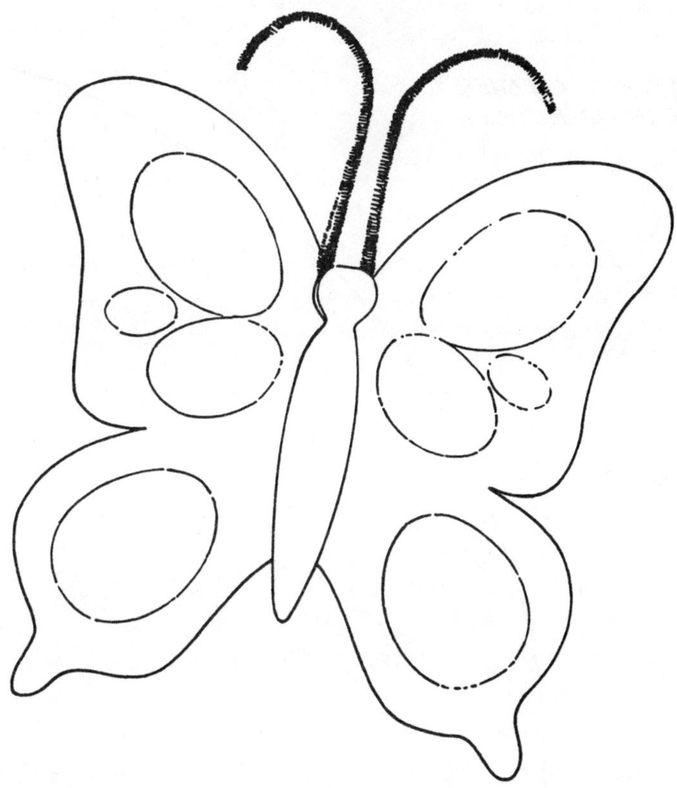

God's Little Summer Creatures

Bring some little summer creatures inside. Display the children's colorful butterflies so everyone can enjoy them.

MATERIALS:

construction paper

black pipe cleaners

scissors

glue

CONSTRUCTION:

1. Reproduce patterns.

2. Trace butterfly onto colored construction paper and cut out.

3. Cut different colored shapes out of construction paper and glue shapes onto the wings.

4. Trace body of the butterfly onto black construction paper and cut out.

5. Take a black pipe cleaner and shape it into the butterfly's antenna.

6. Place the antenna on the head of the butterfly, then fold the head over and glue.

7. Glue body of the butterfly to the wings.

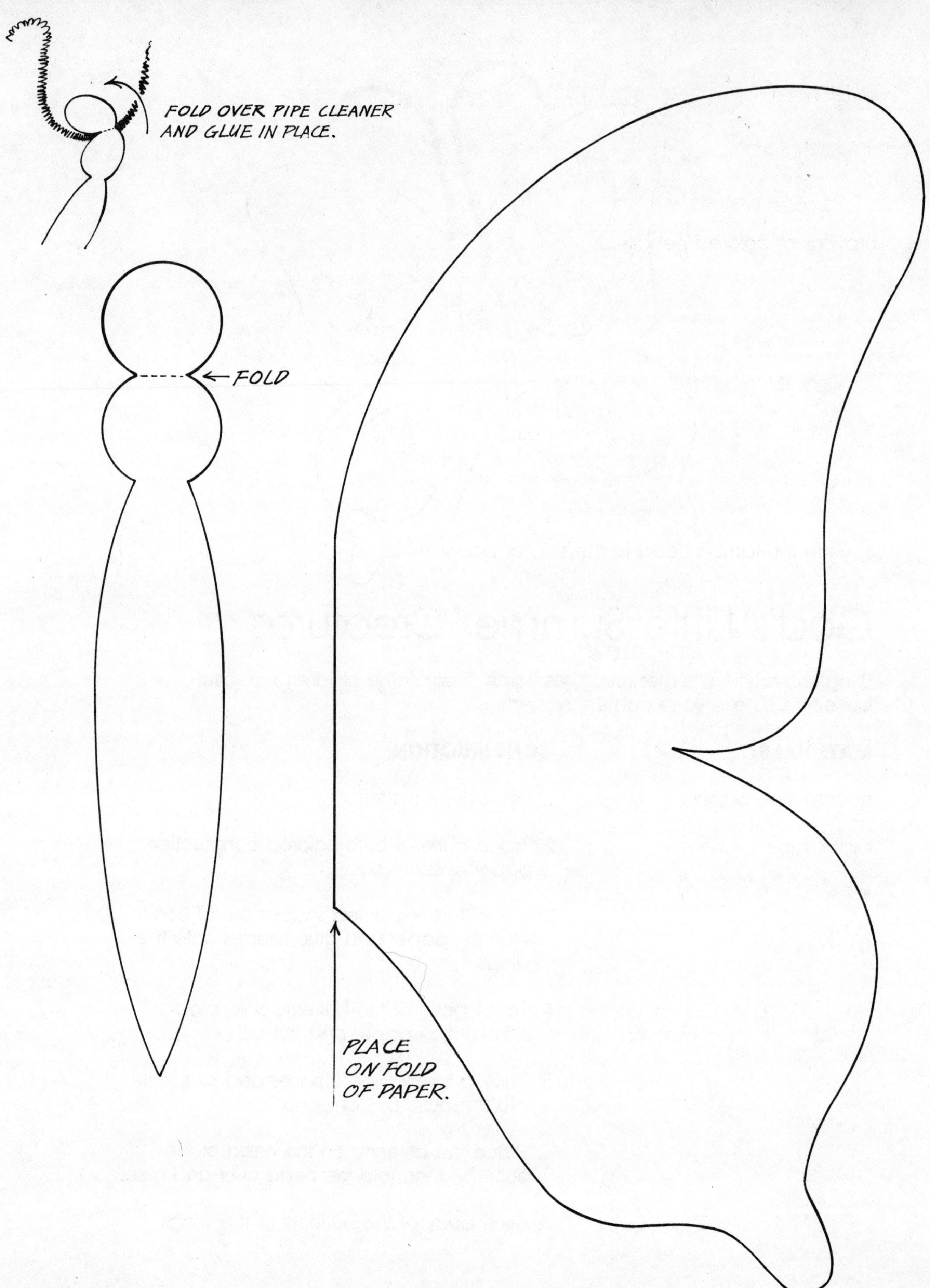

FOLD OVER PIPE CLEANER
AND GLUE IN PLACE.
← FOLD
PLACE
ON FOLD
OF PAPER.

Bible Bookmark

MATERIALS:

construction paper

crayons or colored pencils

scissors

glue

CONSTRUCTION:

1. Reproduce patterns.

2. Have the children draw a face on the
   lamb, color, and cut out.

3. Glue the lamb's head to the strip of paper.

GLUE TAIL HERE.
TAIL
ADD GLUE TO THIS LINE.
ADD GLUE TO THIS LINE.
LEGS - CUT TWO

Little Lamb

This cute, little lamb can be made on the first day of the new Sunday school year or used on the first day of Vacation Bible School. Display the lambs in the classroom. Put the name of the child under the lamb. This will help the children learn one another's name. A larger pattern is provided for the teacher's name. This display can be put on the bulletin board or the classroom door with the teacher's name under it. This will help identify the classroom.

MATERIALS:

construction paper

cotton balls

crayons

scissors

glue

CONSTRUCTION:

1. Reproduce patterns.

2. Color and cut out.

3. Glue head, legs, and tail to the body.

4. Pull cotton balls apart, then glue to the body and to the head of the lamb.

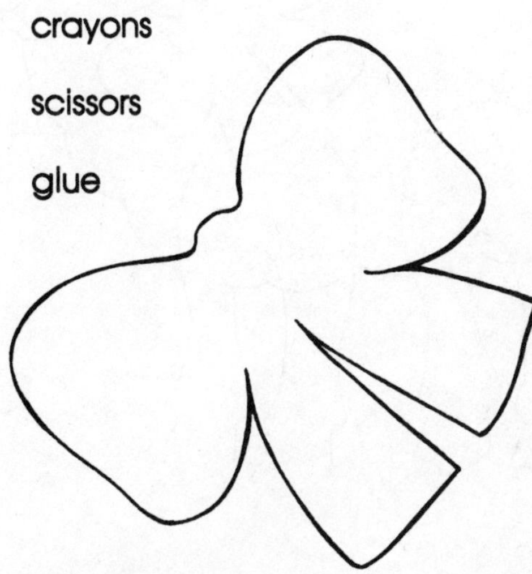

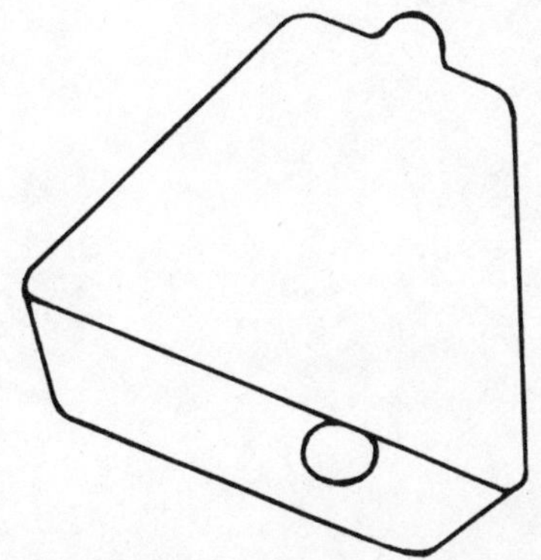

DIAGRAMS FOR
ASSEMBLAGE
GLUE LEGS AND TAIL
TO BACK SIDE OF BODY.
GLUE HEAD AND BOW OR
BELL TO FRONT SIDE.

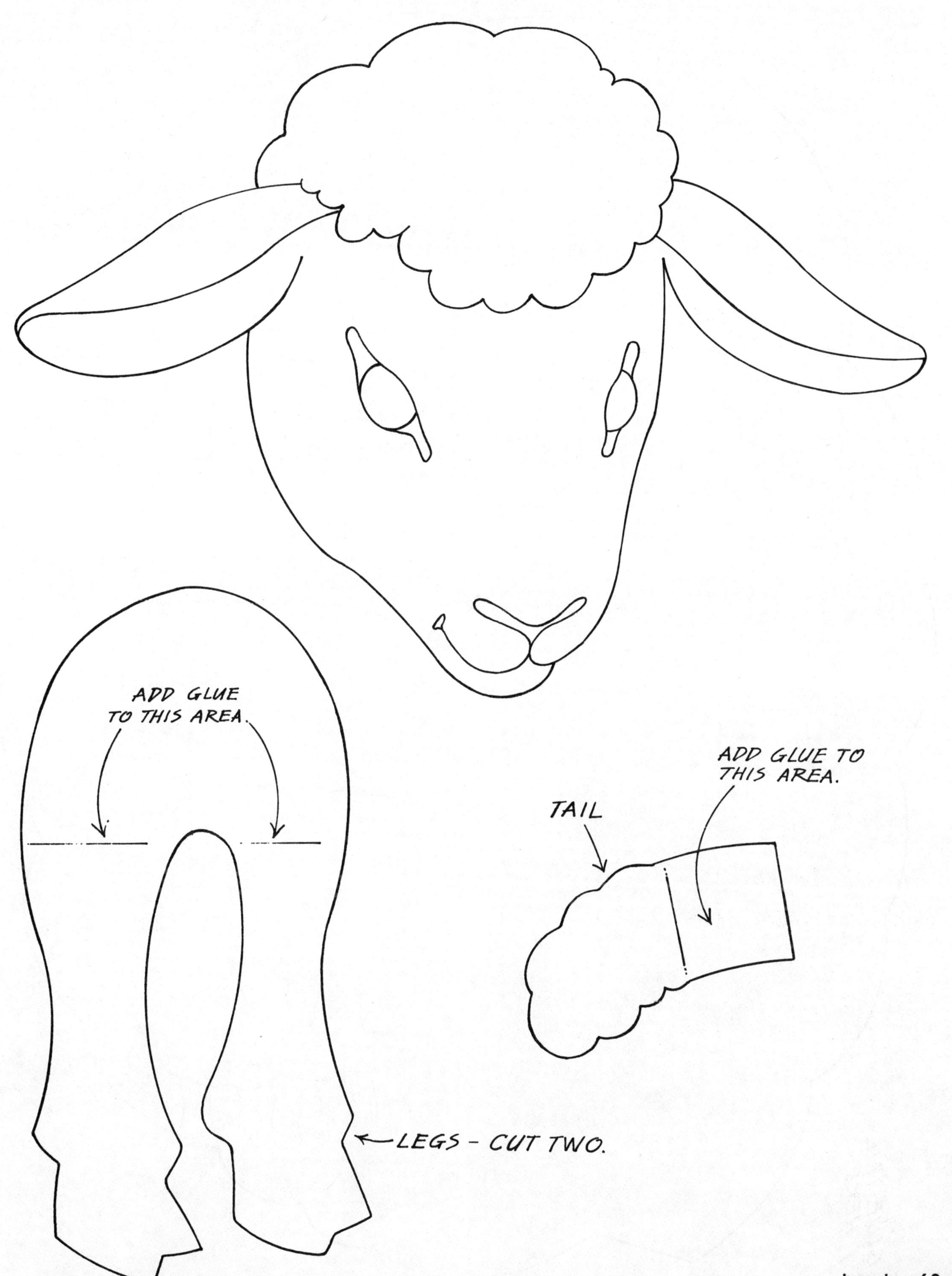

ADD GLUE TO THIS AREA.
ADD GLUE TO THIS AREA.
TAIL
LEGS - CUT TWO.

Lamb 64
GLUE TAIL
HERE.